6079429

WITHDRAWN

D1519461

Population Control Politics

HEALTH, SOCIETY, AND POLICY
a series edited by Sheryl Ruzek and Irving Kenneth Zola

POPULATION CONTROL POLITICS

Women, Sterilization, and Reproductive Choice

THOMAS M. SHAPIRO

 *Temple University Press*
PHILADELPHIA

Temple University Press, Philadelphia 19122
© 1985 by Temple University. All rights reserved
Published 1985
Printed in the United States of America

Library of Congress Cataloging in Publication Data

Shapiro, Thomas M.
    Population control politics.

    (Health, society, and policy)
    Bibliography: p.
    Includes index.
    1. United States—Population policy.   2. Birth control—
Political aspects—United States.   3. Eugenics—Political
aspects—United States.   4. Sterilization of women—United
States.   5. Malthusianism.   6. Population Council (New
York, N.Y.)   I. Title.   II. Series.
HQ766.5.U5S53   1985   304.6'6'0973   84-8681
ISBN 0-87722-365-3

to Ruth

Contents

Preface and Acknowledgments

My interest in this subject began with my involvement with the Committee to End Sterilization Abuse (CESA) in Saint Louis. Within this context of political activism, I started asking the questions that form the basis of this project. I was drawn to CESA for several reasons. My interest logically grew out of my own history of political activism. I was also drawn to working on an issue concerning population control, sterilization abuse, and reproduction rights because it was a concrete way to analyze the theoretical and political dynamics among class, race, and gender.

Decisions about sterilization, particularly among women, reflect the narrow social constraints in which choices about contraception are made. These choices are socially constructed according to larger social, political, and economic objectives. To examine the historical roots and contemporary implications of sterilization and population control, I have asked many broad-ranging questions. In turn, I have had to use archival and historical methods, quantitative data analysis, oral histories, and documentary materials.

Many people have helped me to think and write about population control, sterilization, and reproductive freedom. I want to thank my friends and comrades in CESA for sharing an intense political, intellectual, and human experience. The many courageous women who

came forward to tell their stories of sterilization abuse and to struggle
for justice deserve deep respect. Their passion for justice showed us
the way. In thinking about the movement against sterilization abuse,
the oral histories of key participants have been an invaluable tool. I
am deeply grateful to those women who shared their experiences and
thoughts with me.

The support of the Research and Scholarship Development Fund
and the Research Appointment for Junior Faculty of Northeastern
University are both gratefully acknowledged. In addition, the Department of Sociology and Anthropology awarded me several small
grants to support different phases of the research.

Some of the findings in Chapter 4 have been previously published
in *Social Science and Medicine*. I want to thank my co-authors, William Fisher and Augusto Diana, for their indispensable assistance in
this part of the project.

Many colleagues have offered comments and criticism on one or
more chapters. I thank Wini Breines, Linda Gordon, Lynne Layton,
Lila Leibowitz, Karen Stamm, and Jan Whitaker.

Carla and Richard Birnberg, Ruth Hubbard, Jennifer Schirmer,
and Carmen Sirianni were generous enough to read the entire manuscript and offer thoughtful comments and suggestions.

I thank Michael Ames at Temple University Press for his early
interest in and encouragement of this project, and for his faith and
patience in seeing it to completion.

The work has benefited from two special people. Sheryl Ruzek
went through the manuscript with a fine-tooth comb. Her volumi-
nous and perceptive comments helped clarify many important areas.
Allan Chase shared his enthusiasm, immense knowledge, contacts,
and personal archives. My thinking has come a long way. I am
deeply grateful to all these people who shared their energy, commitment, and intelligence.

Finally, Ruth Birnberg has lived with this project from the beginning. Her encouragement, faith, intelligent insights, emotional support, and love have been essential.

Population Control Politics

1
Birth Control in America: Malthus, Population Control, and the Women's Movement

At age seventeen, living in a foster home, and about to be an unwed mother because she had been raped, Carrie Buck was committed to a hospital. In 1927 Carrie was sterilized; a year later her sister Doris was taken to the Virginia Colony for Epileptics and the Feeble-minded where she, too, was sterilized. In the landmark case of *Buck v. Bell*, Supreme Court Justice Oliver Wendell Holmes, Jr., justified the action in one of the most chilling decisions of our century:

> She may be sexually sterilized without detriment to her general health and that her welfare and that of society will be promoted by her steri-lization. We have seen more than once that the public welfare may call upon the best citizens for their lives. It would be strange if it [the state] could not call upon those who already sap the strength of the State for these lesser sacrifices, often not felt to be such by those concerned, in order to prevent our being swamped with incompe-tence. It is better for all the world, if instead of waiting to execute degenerate offspring for crime, or let them starve for their imbecility, society can prevent those who are manifestly unfit from breeding their kind. . . . Three generations of imbeciles are enough [*Buck v. Bell* 1927].

Doris was married to Matthew Figgins, a plumber and caretaker, for over thirty-eight years. During her childbearing years she and

3

Matthew tried to start a family of their own. She thought the scar on her stomach was the result of an appendectomy and rupture, the explanation she was given for surgery at age sixteen. They anxiously consulted doctors at three hospitals, but none were able to say why she could not have a child. In 1980 Doris Buck Figgins finally learned the reason for her lifelong sadness. "I broke down and cried. My husband and me wanted children desperately. We were crazy about them. I never knew what they'd done to me." She had been "just hurt real bad" to discover that her infertility had been ordered by the state. For years she had felt that she was a failure because she could not have any children, but now she learned it was not her fault (*Washington Post* 1980; *New York Times* 1980). The Buck sisters were sterilized because they were mistakenly thought to be the "feebleminded" daughters of an "antisocial" prostitute. Neither Carrie nor Doris Buck were mentally retarded.

   "I don't remember signing anything. Only when I left the hospital—perhaps an exit paper?" In 1973, nearly fifty years after the Bucks had been sterilized for their alleged "imbecility," Guadalupe Acosta was among a wave of women being sterilized. A month after the delivery, Guadalupe arrived at Los Angeles County Hospital for the standard postnatal checkup. "When I asked the woman doctor [for the Pill], she asked me if I knew what had happened to me." When she replied no, the doctor then explained, "Well, you won't need the Pill because they tied your tubes" (Dreifus 1978, 106–7).
   The physical sterilization of Guadalupe Acosta seems to have resulted in her cultural sterilization as well. A traditional Mexican woman's self-worth and social identity are culturally measured by her ability to bear children, thus affecting her familial network, support groups, and community standing. Guadalupe was one of ten Mexican women who sued the hospital in 1975; one had a saying, "Se me acabó la cancion," literally "My song is finished," which seems to sum up their feelings. The song is the melody of life, which is tied to the ability to procreate (Velez 1978).
   The relationship between Guadalupe and her common-law hus-

band of eight years deteriorated, and she and her two children were forced on welfare when he abandoned them. The others' anguish was similar. Within a few years most had gone through a process of social disengagement: eight relationships suffered irreparable damage and physical punishment of children became more common. They blamed themselves, often expressing their self-anger in vivid nightmares. One dreamt of returning to Mexico without her children and becoming embarrassed when relatives asked where they were; another dreamt that her children had been stolen, killed, and eaten; and one saw her children drowning in lakes.

Guadalupe Acosta and her compatriots were not alone; in a 1974 case, Federal District Judge Gerhard Gesell spoke on behalf of other poor victims of involuntary sterilizations: "Over the last few years, an estimated 100,000 to 150,000 low-income persons have been sterilized annually under federally funded programs." Judge Gesell, in a decision remarkably different from that of Holmes, found that:

> Although Congress has been insistent that all family planning programs function on a purely voluntary basis, there is uncontroverted evidence in the record that . . . an indefinite number of poor people have been improperly coerced into accepting a sterilization operation under the threat that various federally supported welfare benefits would be withdrawn unless they submitted to irreversible sterilization.

Observing that the "dividing line between family planning and eugenics is murky," Judge Gesell ruled that a lack of guidelines to protect patients was "both illegal and arbitrary because they authorize involuntary sterilizations, without statutory or constitutional justification" (*Relf v. Weinberger et al.* 1974). But it was already too late for women like Guadalupe Acosta.

"A surprising request," the doctor thought when a twenty-six year-old native American woman entered his office and asked for a womb transplant. She had been sterilized six years earlier with a complete hysterectomy. At the time she was an alcoholic with two children in foster homes. But now at twenty-six she was no longer an alcoholic. She was in love and planning to marry, and she wanted to raise a family (Marksjarvis 1977)

Dr. Connie Uri, who has conducted an investigation of sterilization practices by the Indian Health Service, sees such sterilizations resulting from "the warped thinking of doctors, who think the solution to poverty is not to allow people to be born. They have the wrong concept of life. They think to have a good life you must be born into a middle-class standard of living" (cited in Marksjarvis 1977). Dr. Uri estimates that the Indian Health Service was sterilizing women at a rate that "could wipe out all pureblood Indian races in less than fifteen years. . . . All the pureblood women of the Kaw tribe of Oklahoma have now been sterilized. At the end of this generation the tribe will cease to exist" (*Medical Tribune,* 1977). According to the account of the twenty-six-year-old sterilized woman, her inability to have children led to divorce. She might be correct in feeling that while her past was taken with a sword and her land with a pen, they had now stolen her future with a scalpel.

Unlike the preceding cases of abuse and coercion, voluntary sterilization is commonplace. In the 1970s there was a dramatic increase in the use of sterilization as a method of contraception. Female sterilization is the most rapidly growing form of birth control in the United States, rising from 200,000 cases in 1970 to over 700,000 in 1980. This threefold increase was aided by government participation through legislative measures, which established family-planning clinics and assisted in payments for sterilizing procedures. While federally funded family planning clinics began operating in 1965, funds for sterilization first became accessible officially in 1971. Sterilization thus became widely available for poor people in a decade that has seen cutbacks in virtually all other public services—and a subsequently reduced standard of living—for the poor. It was also a decade during which abortions became legal, yet were severely restricted for the poor. While abortions have remained at the center of an intense social struggle concerning reproductive freedom and the role of the state in family-planning, sterilizations have been perceived quite differently. Yet sterilization is a significant piece in the puzzle of family-planning politics.

Sterilization is a permanent form of contraception. It involves the disruption of a portion of the male or female reproductive tract so that a sperm can not unite with an ovum. In order to block conception in women the fallopian tubes can be cut, tied, crushed, burned, or blocked by chemicals or occlusive devices. The tubes can be reached by either a vaginal or an abdominal approach. At present five major operative methods are used for female sterilization: laparotomy, minilaparotomy, colpotomy, and the endoscopic methods, laparoscopy and culdoscopy.

An important factor in the spread of female sterilization has been the development of new technologies and procedures like the laparoscope and minilaparotomy, which do not require hospitalization or a general anesthetic. In contrast, vasectomy, or male sterilization, has changed little in two decades and is a simple operation. There are fewer medical complications associated with male than with female sterilization. Among all contraception methods, including abortion, female sterilization has the greatest risk factor. Risk of death for all forms of tubal ligation in the United States is approximately 30 per 100,000. In sharp contrast, no deaths have been reported from vasectomy (Arnold 1978). Recent laparoscopic techniques appear to be safer than other procedures, so the overall mortality risk associated with tubal ligation will probably decrease.

Although sterilization is considered irreversible, some men and women, for various reasons, seek reversal. Experimental procedures using newly developed microsurgical techniques are being tried in an attempt to restore fertility. To date, the results of these procedures, as measured by the achievement of pregnancy, have not been good, and prospects for the future are not encouraging (Plaskon 1982; Population Reports, 1980).

The development of new female sterilization techniques, the intrauterine device, and the pill represent major advances in contraception since World War II. The development of reproductive technology is one aspect of a general trend in American medicine toward increasing dependence on complex technologies (Holmes et al. 1981). Advances in birth control have not been synonymous with the liberation of women, although some women, especially those of better economic and social status, have benefited. But contraceptive technology could, as many believe, be used manipulatively, liberating some women while controlling others.

Technological advances have not typically acted as independent forces to improve the human condition. Social necessity is often the mother of invention, and new advances usually arise from prevailing social structures and cultural attitudes. Reproductive technology has long been used in the United States as a mechanism for social control. At various times in American history fear of blacks, immigrants, native Americans, working people, Hispanics, and welfare recipients has been expressed in explicit, although unofficial, attempts to control their growth rates.

All human groups consciously attempt to regulate their fertility. How, by whom, and for what purposes fertility is regulated is an entirely different—and highly political—matter. A primary consideration is whether population policies instituted in the United States are instruments of domination—policies that function systematically to target poor women, especially those on welfare, for fertility control. Because the topic is controversial, complex, and delicate, it will be helpful to define a few key concepts and to clarify this author's position. *Birth control* may be defined as the more or less voluntary planning and actions by individuals to have the number of children they want and to decide when they want them. Birth control has been practiced since primitive times in all cultures. In the United States, it appeared as early as 1840 as an explicit demand by women (Gordon 1981). From then to the present, birth-control demands have been a cornerstone of the women's rights movement throughout its various phases, although birth control has meant different things at different times. Margaret Sanger pointed to its importance when she said feminism should mean that women must first free themselves from "biological slavery" and this could best be accomplished through birth control (Kennedy 1970).

Family planning represents a different movement. This concept was popularized after World War II by established population organizations like the Planned Parenthood Federation of America. The planned spacing of children was intended to strengthen the nuclear family and, thereby, increase social stability. Family planning represents the incorporation of reproductive control into state programs. Because the concept of family planning was packaged to appeal to the American public and the government, it is laden with ideological assumptions about who should have access to birth control, how a family is defined, and when sex is legitimate. That is, the concept is biased toward a heterosexual, nuclear, married couple, ignoring issues about sexuality altogether. It is decidedly pro-natalist for nuclear families, although preferring small families. Family planning is also the rubric used by public agencies serving women on welfare, who are typically single parents. In this context, family planning has other connotations and is biased in an anti-natalist direction: public agencies, as a rule, do not encourage single parents to plan large families. The relationship between poor people and public agencies in general provides ample grounds for concluding that poor people receive a qualitatively different kind of treatment from the state (Lipsky 1980). The crucial question this raises is to what extent family planning has come to resemble population planning and control.

Population control is used to connote the Malthusian inspired belief that for the good of society, in light of overpopulation, certain groups (usually the least powerful and poor) should reduce their birth rates. Male-dominated elites define the problem and typically seek to impose the solution on women.

Birth control and population planning are not synonymous, although they are often treated as interchangeable. The feminist, eugenics, and socialist movements in the 1920s confused birth control with population control, and much of this confusion still lingers. In the United States, the use of contraceptive devices often varies according to class, gender, and race, indicating that broad social conditions, cultural traditions, and structural inequalities play a large part in shaping a woman's birth control experience. Middle-class women are encouraged to use methods, such as the diaphram and the pill, that allow individual control. Poor women are encouraged to use methods, such as the intrauterine device and sterilization, that are controlled by physicians. In many places, abortion is accessible only to those who can pay for it. Among most minority groups, women, rather than men, are sterilized; among white, middle-class, married couples there is a higher proportion of vasectomies. Ninety-eight percent of Medicaid sterilizations are performed on women (Gerzowski et al. 1981).

This book is a critique of discriminatory population-control practices in the United States. However, the author believes that families and individuals should have access to the broadest range of contraceptive services available, and they should regulate their reproduction to suit their best interest. The rights to plan a family, without losing the freedom to enjoy a full sexual life, and to control decisions over one's body are dependent on the ability to regulate fertility by contraception. If contraception fails because of technological inadequacy or failure to meet a woman's basic needs, abortion must be available to regulate fertility. This book is not an attack on birth control; rather, it is a critique of how the need for reproductive health services became translated into the delivery of population control–infused programs of family planning. Hence, the system developed with the contradictory aspects of a program based on egalitarian aspirations, but with services premised on fundamentally antidemocratic population-control objectives. While public family-planning programs are no substitute for social justice, they still deliver a level of reproductive health care that might otherwise be unavailable, even if these programs bear the stamp of population control. A striking paradox calls for an explanation: how is it that sterilization has become a vehicle both for social control and for liberation? This paradox highlights a crucial dilemma with which feminists have been grappling. Rosalind Petchesky writes in *Abortion and Woman's Choice* that one feminist tendency is to emphasize the individual dimensions of reproduction and the individual's right to choose. Another tendency emphasizes the social dimensions, the historically determined social needs of women as a group, and the "socialization of responsibility." According to Petchesky, the dilemma here is philosophical as well as practical and strategic (Petchesky 1984).

Attempts at population control invariably target women. Cultural attitudes toward women are closely intertwined with attempts to control population; thus gender is a critical dimension of analysis. Clitoridectomy, for example, was performed to check "woman's mental disorder," beginning in America in the late 1860s and lasting until perhaps the mid-1920s (Barker-Benfield 1976). Female circumcision coexisted with and then superseded clitoridectomy and lasted until about 1937. Both operations were performed to check what was thought to be "a growing epidemic of female masturbation, an activity which men feared inevitably aroused women's naturally boundless but usually repressed sexual appetite for men" (Barker-Benfield 1976, 120–21). These practices seem extreme and outrageous today, but they are indicative of what medical practices and prevailing cultural attitudes toward women and sexuality were like for at least three-quarters of a century.

Similar attitudes became institutionalized within the medical profession. The increasing complexity of contraceptive (and childbearing) technologies has placed major decisions about their development and use in the hands of medical professionals; women, the primary consumers, are inadequately informed and thus dependent on professional expertise. The appropriation of the childbirth process, for instance, has placed a female function in the hands of a profession heavily dominated by male ideology. Consequently, women's knowledge of, and control over, their bodies has diminished while that of the medical profession has increased (Smart and Smart 1978). The transition from midwives to gynecologists and obstetricians brought a host of medical practices based on sexist cultural attitudes that resulted in new horrors for women (Ehrenreich and English 1973). Julius Roth notes that professional training does not necessarily succeed in creating a universalistic moral neutrality. On the contrary, it is safer "to assume that those engaged in dispensing professional services . . . will apply the evaluation of social worth common to their culture" (Roth 1974, 500).

Population control objectives are focused on women, specifically to limit female fertility over a reproductive life span. In contrast, birth control—given conventional American norms about sexual activity—could be directed toward either males or females. The main thrust of technological developments and programs that focus on women is supplied by social, cultural, and political assumptions rather than biological determinants. Because there are no biological reasons for directing birth control efforts at women instead of men, historical, social, and cultural influences must be identified. One of the central themes is the conflict between population control and the women's struggle to control their own reproductive capacity. Many feel that population-control programs appropriate a major aspect of female gender identity by placing it in the hands of those who design policies, develop technologies, and construct programs that are used on or against women and their bodies (Bram 1978). This view sees women as the targets of population-planning programs and often as the "victims" of these efforts. Karen Michaelson, for instance, argues: "Even as contraceptive technology has developed, it has been applied not to give women greater control over their own reproductive lives, but to give others control over women's entire life circumstances" (Michaelson 1981, 25). If one is to take this view seriously, it is vital to ask whether such programs exist in the United States, how they came into existence, what social motives are behind them, and how the delivering organizations work.

The history of population control and the struggle for reproductive rights is far richer than a mere unfolding of economic forces or the playing out of political ideologies. This history becomes a complex and impassioned enterprise when it focuses on the growth and development of the respective social movements—each of which takes shape through individuals and organizations who act powerfully in its behalf—attempting to define reality. Such an approach helps to reveal the internal complexities and contradictions of population policy in the United States.

Historically, reproduction control in the United States has had various, and often contradictory, sources of support. Three schools of thought have shaped the nation's attitudes toward birth control. The *women's movement*, throughout most phases, has stood for birth control and reproductive freedom as a social precondition for sexual equality, even if the meaning of birth control has changed. *Eu-*

genicists have been concerned about alleged social disorganization spread by the rapid growth of racial and ethnic minorities. Further deterioration of an endangered American stock, threatened by immigration and by prolific reproduction within, can be prevented by curtailing breeding. The worries of *population controllers* are more class oriented. They are concerned about "overpopulation" among the lower classes and poorer nations and its impact on the environment, food supplies, and the nation's political stability. The interests of the women's movement, the eugenicists, and the population controllers are socially remote from one another, and they historically vie for dominance. Tracing these three positions is not simple because the lines are neither linear nor distinct; instead, they tend to crisscross and become blurred. At times these three schools have cooperated with one another, but their coalitions were fragile. These were pragmatic attempts to maximize one group's influence over the others in the belief that the spread of contraceptive practices would promote its goals, even if motives had to be disguised.

The history of birth control in the United States reveals two broadly differing sets of motives: those who want to make reproductive services available as a right, a matter of health, and a necessary condition for sexual equality; and those who want to use fertility control to preserve their institutional interests. The key questions are: to what extent are sterilizations the delivery of a wanted service, and to what extent do they represent an "acceptable" policy of population control targeted at curtailing the fertility of the poor?

Population control is the basis for most modern programs of family-planning, and these programs are premised on the original work of Thomas Malthus, the influential British political economist whose most famous work was published in 1798 (Malthus 1967). Perhaps no other pseudo-scientific doctrine has been as durable as Malthusianism. Two principles are fundamental to the doctrine: the number of people grows geometrically while the food supply increases only arithmetically. Malthus had no evidence that this is true. In addition, his formula for disaster did not foresee qualitative leaps in modern agricultural production (Simon 1981) or differential population growth rates or a parental preference for fewer children

(Schultz 1982). Malthus did not recognize either that women had practiced contraception for centuries (Gordon 1976) or that each new person represents not only another mouth to feed but also another pair of hands to help produce. Malthus also seemed to confuse the production of food with its highly inequitable consumption. Despite a lack of basis in historical fact, Malthusianism has continued to flourish as an integral part of the general corpus of biological-determinist thought.

Malthusians have emphasized Malthus's first principle of exponential population growth. Thus a major thrust of population controllers has been to achieve some sort of fertility control to slow down, even arrest, these growth rates. Modern population controllers have added a new twist since the late 1960s. They argue that the human race is outgrowing the planet's capacity to support it. This view claims that there are certain physical limitations of nonrenewable resources, such as fossil fuels, minerals and arable land, and resources whose renewal rate is a fixed physical property of nature (fresh water) and that these are rapidly being consumed by a growing population. No economic system, no matter how rational or efficient, can create minerals, make the earth bigger, or find fresh water where none exists (World Agriculture Research Project 1969). This argument has added fresh urgency, vitality, and new converts to Malthusianism (Ehrlich 1968; Chase 1977).

Population control thus takes the domain assumption that over-population erodes economic growth, causes poverty, depletes resources, and degrades environmental quality. In this view, over-population is caused by a failure to use sexual restraint; a shortage of birth-control technologies, information, and services; or a lack of motivation to use available methods and services. Malthusians and Neo-Malthusians, although united in their goals, have profoundly disagreed on policy questions and methods for achieving these goals. Malthus was opposed to contraception, which he considered a vice; he relied, instead, on the power of moral persuasion and the fear of God. Neo-Malthusians, on the contrary, were early advocates of contraception, which they view as an essential tool in arresting over-population. An important distinction is that Malthusians depend on morality and ideology to curb fertility growth while Neo-Malthusians rely on science and government services.

Overpopulation, a core concept of population control, is devoid of specific meaning outside its ideological context. The image is one of overcrowding, but clearly something else is meant. Densely populated Western, industrialized societies like Holland are not said to be overpopulated but sparsely populated nations like Brazil are. The term is applied only to poorer nations, regardless of population size, growth rate, density, or resource base. The term implies a relationship between population and level of production, explaining poverty and "underdevelopment" by asserting that there are too many people. Massive and persistent unemployment is invariably blamed on overpopulation. In some areas of the world, population size is part of a larger complex of problems, exacerbating anxiety over food, energy, space, and other physical properties of the earth as well as increasing tension about the unequal distribution of resources and wealth. The important point, however, is that overpopulation is not the only or even the main cause of poverty (Simon 1981; George 1977; Perelman 1977). Overpopulation can be seen as a social condition of poverty, and both are products of inequalities in a social system (George 1977; Lappe and Collins 1977).

Perhaps there is a historical parallel that mirrors the split between Malthusians and Neo-Malthusians of the late 1800s and between today's population controllers and the New Right. Because it is opposed to intervention in private matters, the New Right wants the government out of the business of family, sex, and birth control. The New Right, akin to Malthus, proposes a massive re-infusion of moral rectitude and ideological control to compel responsibility. Furthermore, it does not want the state to help those who do not conform to their notions of morality, sexuality, and the family. Population controllers are the modern-day Neo-Malthusians, historically and ideologically. Thus, while population controllers and the New Right have similar goals, they, like Malthusians and Neo-Malthusians, have opposing views of the state's role in family planning and contraception, as Malthusians and Neo-Malthusians have historically stood in opposition on these questions. Since the mid-1960s, sections of the

women's movement have advocated state assistance in birth control
and contraception. This convergence of interests between segments
of the women's movement and population controllers has produced a
fragile, pragmatic alliance that the New Right threatens to disrupt by
attacking publicly supported family-planning efforts.

Paul Ehrlich's *Population Bomb* and Garrett Hardin's writings
about "lifeboat ethics" have been instrumental in popularizing overpopulation as a global peril (Ehrlich 1968; Hardin 1968). The United
States, through the World Bank, the U.S. Agency for International
Development (A.I.D.), and other agencies, has strongly encouraged, at times compelled, Third World countries to limit their rates
of population growth (Mass 1976; Demerath 1976). Much has been
written about the relationship between population, development, and
resources, especially as it constrains the developing world. A generally accepted strategy for alleviating problems associated with population growth rests on controlling rates of growth. Sterilization, outside the United States, is a favored solution pushed by international
and U.S. agencies. For example, A.I.D. has worked with medical
equipment manufacturers to develop laparoscopes suitable for use in
developing countries. A.I.D. also funded research for the development of tubal clips and bands (Population Reports, 1978).

In contrast, however, little (Littlewood 1977; Bachrach and
Bergman 1973) has been written about the impact of similar overpopulation themes on domestic thinking and policy in the United
States. Dramatic cuts in public expenditures (aimed at social programs) are likely to produce even more pressure to limit growth rates
of groups that are perceived as a burden on the public purse. Biological determinism, which underlies yesterday's eugenicists and today's
population controllers and New Right, is rising again, as it always
does in times of economic trouble and retrenchment of domestic
expenditures.

An important set of issues must be addressed: how Malthusianism functions as an ideology, how it is used to manipulate public
sentiment, how it is a response to political and economic pressures,
the interests it represents, and the different forms it can take. Ideas,
whether based on reality or not, can motivate individual, group, or

societal behavior. But no set of ideas can be communicated and imposed by words alone. How people interpret the world around them
is influenced by the ideas propagated by dominant groups. But even
so, people do not merely, or without question, believe what they are
told. Ideas take root only if they are consistent with social life as
people experience it or if they provide a reasonable explanation of
social phenomena, and they can be sustained only if they continue to
be confirmed by social experience (Piven and Cloward 1982). Notions of population control influenced American social policy in the
past, most notably in the 1920s and also in 1930s. These were troubled
eras during which the Malthusian-inspired solutions of restrictive
immigration control and eugenic sterilization became palatable, even
sensible, to broad segments of the American population.

Curtailing the fertility of selected subgroups or classes is the goal
of Malthusian-based programs. Fertility control has appealed to policy makers because fertility appears to be the most easily manipulated variable with which to alleviate problems, such as poverty
and inequality. Furthermore, it offers a solution to social problems
through altering the behavior of the poor rather than redistributing
power or resources. President Reagan, for example, declared that
unemployment exists not only because of the recession, but also because "the work force is so big" (*Boston Globe* 1982).

Historically, in a number of societies, population control has taken
the form of a set of ideas expressing desired policy outcomes that
clearly appeals to and serves the interests of those who want to preserve their dominant positions of wealth, power, and status. Therefore, it is vital to ask if contemporary population control solutions are
the carefully nurtured and aggressively pushed ideas of identifiable
groups of people with specific interests. The Neo-Malthusian thesis
corresponds less to reality than to a conscious or unconscious ideological position. The solutions are characterized by a kind of population fetishism—the consideration of the population variable itself,
abstracted from a framework of complex relationships. Embedded in
this fetishism is the twin notion that the complex factors accounting
for human reproductive behavior can be first isolated and measured
and then manipulated.

The following thesis will be examined: changes in the state's role in promoting contraception, abortion, and sterilization correspond to the shifting interests and strategies of the dominant groups in society, as well as to changing social conditions. This is a perspective in the sociological tradition of examining how America's capitalist class attempts to dominate public policy (Zeitlin 1980; Domhoff 1979; Useem 1984). Members of this class—owners, managers, and directors of large corporations—naturally try to ensure the survival of the present form of society and their privileged positions in its social structure. Members of the capitalist class, acting mainly through philanthropic organizations, articulate a strategy of population planning consistent with the needs of capitalist society. Further, their conception of fertility control contains a strong component of population control. They believe that family-planning goals will benefit the society as a whole, just as they believe that the private accumulation of wealth and private decisions about how to use that wealth and its income are in the best interests of society. A two-stage process is conceptualized: farsighted, leading members of the class first attempt to socialize other members and other elites to the values of population control; second, they translate that consciousness into a generalized ideology and then pressure the state to formulate policies of population control. The effect of this intervention is the transformation of the potentials of birth control and the need and desire for contraception into publicly assisted programs of population control.

A major achievement of the capitalist class has been to incorporate population policy within the welfare state. This achievement institutionalizes the population control motives of an elite and makes their interests appear universal. It also shifts the financial, organizational and ideological burden for population control from private endeavors and charitable contributions to public agencies and taxpayer support. In the process population policy is rationalized, allowing for a greater degree of coordination and planning. Finally, it signifies the acceptance of population control assumptions at the public level; no longer are they merely privately held views about the world.

Dialectically, this shift has far-reaching theoretical and practical implications. It transfers the focus of analysis from the direct plans of a specific class to the complex, sometimes inconsistent mechanisms of the modern welfare state. Population-control activities, indeed nearly its whole agenda, prior to the mid-1960s can be traced in a fairly linear fashion to elite sources and concerns. Examples include immigration restriction laws, above all the Johnson Act of 1924; eugenic statutes in thirty states, between 1907 and 1931, to sterilize the "unfit"; the promulgation of a Malthusian ideology equating social problems, poverty, and unemployment with large families among the poor; and charitable enterprises to bring contraception to the masses. Since the mid-1960s population-planning strategy has become more rationalized, centralized, planned, bureaucratically administered, and, supposedly, universal. The welfare state is responsible for programs and services that were once private. Thus the focus changes from examining capitalist class activities and motives to analyzing the development and function of the modern welfare state, thus diverting attention from the influence of the capitalist class. The shift is both strategic and substantive, although there seems to be more change in style and scale than in content or interests served. But the changes are not merely cosmetic because some important changes have occurred. Millions are now served by public programs, in contrast to the experimental, small-scale and haphazard application of private programs. Previously, the needs of population-control targets were structurally precluded, but this is no longer the case.

To understand this theoretical formulation, one must examine two closely related societal developments: health care and welfare politics. Contraception, increasingly medical, has become a commodity, and public family-planning programs are within the health-care domain; thus one must attain a theoretical grasp of the institutional interests in health-care politics. Robert Alford identifies dominant structural interests as "those served by the structure of social, economic, and political institutions as they exist at any given time" (Alford 1975, 14). The monopoly of the medical profession and the dominance of large pharmaceutical firms are obvious. But the hegemony of their interests, and those of business, is challenged by what Alford calls "corporate rationalizers," that is, professional

health planners and researchers, public health agencies, cost-efficiency experts, and even some hospital administrators. Corporate
rationalizers attempt to better distribute medical resources, health
care opportunities and human resources. The interests of Medicaid
clients, family planning service clients, and women are called "repressed" because "no social institutions or political mechanisms in
the society insure that these interests are served" (Alford 1975, 15).
Furthermore, these interests will not be served unless extraordinary
political energies are mobilized to offset the intrinsic disadvantages
of their situation. Planning and delivery of fertility-control policies
cannot be seen as a direct process from capitalist-class plans to specific outcomes. Rather, it is a very complex process that involves fil-
tering and intermingling of multiple interests, even though the dominant structural interests strongly influence policy objectives.

The second development is the growth and function of the modern welfare state. At one level the welfare state cushions the most
severe impact of the economic system by acknowledging the need for
services to aid those who are economically deprived. More broadly
than aiding the poor, millions of women have gained access to contraceptive services and reproductive health care that, without state
aid, would have been costly or unavailable. In general, welfare programs represent small victories and concessions to the poor people
who use them to sustain an essential standard of living.

At another level, many analysts contend that the key to understanding social welfare is in its support of the larger political, economic and social order (Piven and Cloward 1971; Wilson 1977;
Lipsky 1980; Schirmer 1982). The modern welfare state, instead of
equalizing outcomes or bringing about social change, reproduces the
prevailing social values and stratification of the larger society. Preserving social stability and control means maintaining hierarchies of
gender, class, and race. This occurs because welfare state policies
are a set of values supporting the prevailing notions about work, society, the family, and women.

Rosalind Petchesky contributes a crucial feminist dimension to
this understanding. She writes that efforts to control fertility also in-
volve control over sexuality and the physical health of women, the

terms and social conditions of contraception and motherhood, and the structure of the family. In addition, "Strategies of fertility control are responses to popular practices and changing ideologies about fertility" (Petchesky 1984, 26). Women have argued for a long time that contraceptive and reproductive health-care issues bridge personal and political interests. There should be no quarrel with this proposition any longer because welfare policies that define appropriate sexuality, set the terms and conditions of contraception and motherhood, and regulate family life and fertility transform private concerns into public interests, and personal matters into political issues. The furthest reaches of the welfare state define the state's boundaries of social control. The welfare state breaches the barriers between private affairs and public responsibility.

The welfare state has a dual, and apparently contradictory, nature. Acknowledging major defects of the private economic system, it provides some essential social services. These programs simultaneously function as mechanisms for social control because they are designed to preserve larger social values and interests. While the welfare state institutionalizes gender, class, and race hierarchies, it also creates and sustains the power of a stratum of professional monopolists, corporate rationalizers, policy planners and research professionals, and administrators.

The transformation from private activities to public commitment carries a legitimizing force. The welfare state is not monolithic, however, and it carries seeds of change that were not present before. The welfare state institutionalizes dominant elite and professional interests, but, dialectically, this same process legitimizes the expressions, hitherto repressed, of social needs by women, minorities, and the poor—to express their social needs. Groups and interests that were once structurally precluded are now included, although they are repressed and intrinsically disadvantaged. Once social welfare programs are established, the amount and availability of services becomes an immediate issue for clients. Under certain conditions, the nature and content of services can become a basis on which programs can be challenged by clients. The irony is that the welfare state collects repressed individuals into groups and potentially defines common grounds of grievance. The welfare state targets itself for collective action. But the same process that legitimizes clients' collective grievances also limits the boundaries of conflict to specific programs and services or, broadly, to social welfare. The interests of clients are structurally accounted for—legitimated but repressed. Saying that the welfare state is not monolithic is not to be confused with implying that the state is democratic or that the state can be influenced equally by any number of parties. Alford reminds us that extraordinary political energies must be mobilized for repressed interests to break through. Collective action, once it occurs, is channeled to immediate programs. If minorities, welfare mothers, or the poor protest, the target normally is the welfare system, not the economic system or patriarchy.

This study offers a concrete exploration of several, more abstract tensions inherent in the welfare state. There are tensions between social-service and social-control functions. The implicit promise of equal opportunity conflicts with policies that maintain social and economic hierarchies. Organized social movements that attempt to define reality and gain concessions clash with the limits of reform within the welfare state framework. An examination of how and why the execution of population policy objectives was transformed from the capitalist class to the welfare state, and the ramifications of that change, is central to this analysis; thus it will be helpful to explore notions about general population policy.

Bachrach and Bergman suggest that the overall objective of American population policy should be to produce opportunities for better conditions of life for any given segment and for society as a whole (Bachrach and Bergman 1973). Population policy can be conceptualized as "political decisions that have legal status and are aimed at influencing the size, growth, nongrowth or composition of the population of some political unit" (Kammeyer 1975, 375). This formulation implies that the actions—decrees, laws, regulations, administrative orders, or operating procedures—of some political authority are a conscious, deliberate, and explicit attempt to influence population. However, there are often policy decisions that, although not intended to do so, affect the population. For example, federal housing programs since World War II have benefited middle- and upper-class families with children, but have made suitable housing less accessible to low-income families with children (Commission on Population Growth and the American Future 1972, 157). Other laws have contradictory effects on population growth, thus there is neither a consistent, systematic pronatal nor antinatal plan.

Further complicating an uncluttered notion of population policy, according to Kammeyer, is "the tendency of governmental authorities to disguise what are, *in fact*, population policies as something else" (Kammeyer 1975, 376). One example of disguising explicit policies may have been the pre-*Roe v. Wade* (1973) pressures to liberalize abortion laws. Such pressures were, at least in part, the response of many legislators and policy elites to the perceived excessive fertility of the population, especially among unmarried welfare recipients. Another example is the proffering of sterilization availability under the rubric of reproductive health care at a time when most health services (and others) are being scaled down or eliminated for the poor. A policy that is aimed at decreasing the population or changing its character, particularly if it is aimed at a defined segment, will be viewed with apprehension by the population and thus pursued gingerly by political leaders.

A single unified population policy has never existed in the United States. Congress and the executive branch have side-stepped every opportunity to impose a direct, coordinated population policy on a pluralistic society; policies toward children, for example, have always been a contradictory mixture of pronatalism and antinatalism. One explicit population policy in the United States was that of racist immigration quotas adopted in the 1920s. A more recent attempt at explicit population-policy making is the immigration bill that has been in Congress since the early 1980s. One notable provision in this proposed legislation is the imposition, for the first time, of fines on employers who hire illegal aliens. The assumption is that if employers face sanctions for hiring them, they will decline to do so. Employment opportunities for illegal aliens would then decline, and the flow of undocumented workers into the country would be reduced.

Bachrach and Bergman posit that the United States has a limited population-policy discourse emphasizing the manipulation of human fertility and is preoccupied with the creation of public policies facilitating more effective manipulation of human reproductive behavior. American population policy is based on a family-planning model. This confinement of the discourse, an intentional consequence, was designed by the dominant policy makers who form the American Population Coalition, which has the Population Council at its center and is linked to groups like Planned Parenthood and the Association for Voluntary Sterilization (AVS). Founded by the Rockefeller family in 1952, the Population Council has been a primary shaper of American population policy from that time until the present. The Planned Parenthood Federation of America, founded in 1942, grew out of the feminist birth control movement of the 1920s and 1930s, especially Margaret Sanger's strategy to gain acceptance and eventual legality for birth control by deferring to professional leadership and the medical profession. AVS was formed in 1937 and represents the narrow focus of advocating sterilization to contain fertility. The histories and legacies of these organizations are important not only for population policy and attitudes about sexuality, but also for public family-planning programs and sterilization. Following Bachrach and Bergman's lines of analysis, it is important to explore further the basis of this coalition, how much influence it wields, how that power is translated into public policy, what policy objectives are pursued, and what social interests these groups represent. In addition to understanding the power of this coalition, it is important to assess the impact of other potential power groups, such as the medical profession, the church, and family-planning bureaucrats.

Extraordinary political energies have been mobilized since the early 1970s by feminist groups, such as the National Organization for Women, the Committee to End Sterilization Abuse, the National Abortion Rights Action League, the Reproductive Rights National Network, the Committee to Defend Reproductive Rights, the Feminist Health Centers, the Committee for Abortion Rights and Against Sterilization Abuse and others in an attempt to break through a closed policy discourse, which had been limited to elites and professionals. To the extent that a breakthrough has occurred, not only by feminists but also by Right-to-Life groups and the New Right, population policy has become more open, more public, and, above all, more political.

The growth component of population policy has been coupled to a family-planning model of procreation, contraception, and sexuality. The ideological attractiveness of a family-planning model, which isolates reproductive concerns and relies on technological solutions, as a method to pursue wider population policy formulations, seems apparent. This strategy envisions the achievement of population limitation, and a corresponding reduction of instability, insecurity, and poverty without substantial change in the distributions of power within social and economic institutions. Despite its recognition of the need for widespread change, the Commission on Population Growth and the American Future, the first commission established by the president and Congress to examine population growth and its impact, limited its proposals to the areas of population growth and fertility control. Thus, "In order to permit freedom of choice," the blue-ribbon commission recommended "that all administrative restrictions on access to voluntary contraceptive sterilization be eliminated so that the decision be made solely by physician and patient" (Commission on Population Growth and the American Future 1972, 171). There was a clear unwillingness of leadership to go beyond the technology-medical approach.

Since the commission's report, population policy—especially family-planning, welfare, and immigration components—has become highly political. A political analysis framing notions of population policy within major structural changes in American society in the past two to three decades, which this book develops, will clarify the social motives behind current population politics and why population restrictions may have appeal.

Female sterilization—risky, controversial, and irreversible—is federally financed for the poor; thus, this author uses it as a logical method with which to test the penetration and domination of a population-control ideology on family-planning programs. Detailed examination of two questions is required to confirm the thesis that the incidence and prevalence of sterilization reflect the dominance of population control on family-planning policies in the United States. First, do significant racial and/or class based differentials exist? Second, if systematic discrimination exists, is it the logical and desired result of social policies and programs and the manner in which these services are delivered? The issue of possible discrimination has been addressed, but reports claiming its nonexistence are so seriously flawed methodologically that they are inadequate and inappropriate. Analysis of information from an appropriate data source enables one to draw a valid and accurate portrait of sterilization patterns.

Population Control Politics will proceed according to the following plan. Chapter 2 traces the various influences on birth control in American history, highlighting the legacies of the eugenics, birth-control and population-control movements. Chapter 3 links these historical legacies to the present by looking at the thinking and influence of the Population Council, which has been identified as one of the most dominant population organizations. Chapter 4 is the empirical centerpiece of the book. The author has used the best data available, The National Survey on Family Growth, which is virtually untapped on this subject, to construct the contemporary pattern of female sterilization and to explore competing explanations. Chapter 5 analyzes the differential pattern of sterilization in terms of physicians' attitudes regarding the sexuality of women on welfare, cultural attitudes, the practices of agencies delivering public services, and broader social policy. The movement against sterilization abuse— its origins, politics, strategy, and impact—is explained in Chapter 6. Chapter 7 establishes the contemporary social context of population policy. It examines the possible conjuncture between the politics of the moment and fundamental structural transformations that underlie America's changing attitudes and policies about population growth and birth control, family planning, and, particularly, population control. Finally, the discussion of sterilization is used to reflect on the functions of the modern welfare state and to consider the complex configuration of gender, class, and race in American society.

The disappointments of Doris Buck or Guadalupe Acosta, as well as the substantial number of other women who later regretted having been sterilized, may seem frivolous in a world where people die in senseless wars, malnutrition retards the physical and mental growth of millions of children, and fear of nuclear holocaust is a growing reality. However, if a public power imposes sterilization on poor women in the name of an ideology advanced to control the poor and to cut future welfare costs, then sterilization must be seen both as an attempt by the state to regulate the terms of family life and as a repressive weapon in a war against the poor.

2

The Dark Side of Reproductive "Choice": Influences on Population Control in American History

Civilization's going to pieces. . . . Have you read "The Rise of the Colored Empires" by this man Goddard? The idea is if we don't look out the white race will—will be utterly submerged. It's all scientific stuff; it's been proved. . . . It's up to us, who are the dominant race, to watch out or these other races will have control of things.

Tom Buchanan in *The Great Gatsby*

STERILIZATION HAS a long history in America. Throughout its history, which stretches over one hundred years, the movement has been characterized by periods of ascendance and descendance (Paul 1968). Each time the movement resurfaces, it does so with fresh social grounding; therefore, in each period it appears in a slightly different social context. In the American historical setting of underpopulation, the need for an expanding labor force, and massive immigration, class, ethnic, and racial lines are often blurred. While the major topic of this analysis is sterilization, it is only one method—a most effective one—of population control. Underlying population control is a set of ideas and practices that posit the inherent superiority of one group over another. These claims of superiority usually rest on racial, gender, ethnic, or class appeals. Only in recent decades, as in the case of China, has population control been attempted on a more uniform and equitable, although Draconian, basis. Be-

29

cause the history of a problem is an aspect of the problem itself (Goldmann 1969), an examination of the origins and legacies of population control and sterilization should reveal insights and enhance our contemporary understanding.

In the United States there has been a durability in the social motives and social forces supporting population control and in the social settings that have nurtured the "sciences" supporting such ideas. Furthermore, a continuous if uneven development can be traced throughout population control's history in America—tactics have changed, not the basic social or political orientation. An organizational continuity likewise can be traced from its early eugenic basis to modern day population control groups. While ideas and organizations are often shaped to fit the tenor of the times, solutions have remained remarkably similar. Prior to a discussion of twentieth-century developments in the United States, the scientific and intellectual underpinnings of population control should be highlighted. This chapter does not purport to rewrite the history of America's population control, eugenic, or sterilization movements. In fact, it draws heavily on reliable, authoritative accounts (Ludmerer 1972; Haller 1963; Chase 1977; Higham 1965; Hofstadter 1959). These accounts are supplemented with original historical materials in areas that are particularly relevant to this examination.

Thomas Malthus (1766–1834)

Thomas Malthus is widely considered to be one of the world's great thinkers. Certainly, his work is the bedrock inspiration for population control. His reputation is, perhaps, ironic. He was a Christian minister, yet his name is associated with a cruel and dour mechanical doctrine of despair. He was an influential economist who knew very little about demographic theory (there was very little to know about). Nonetheless, his name is ineradicably associated with the subject of population and population control. His legacy is at once a moral prescription about capitalist and sexual values. Malthus's famous 1798 work, *An Essay on Population*, claimed that population growth would always prevent "the future improvement" of society. Addressed to the radical thinkers of the Enlightenment, the essay opposed their belief that it was possible to create a better society. A scientific analysis of social relationships proved conclusively that "the perfectability of the mass of mankind" was a hopeless illusion. His essay was a spirited defense against English workingmens' societies and their Jacobin traditions of self-education, republicanism, and a radical perspective on economic, political, and religious institutions (Schwendinger and Schwendinger 1974).

Malthus's defense of the landed aristocracy and the status quo was organized around ecological relationships, demographic trends, and individual morality. The human species possesses the "instinct" to propagate at the rate of doubling its size every twenty-five years. At this rate it would rapidly outstrip the available food supply. His famous dictum, for which there is no empirical evidence, is that population increases exponentially while subsistence increases only arithmetically. According to Malthus, unless population is held in check by certain "natural forces," masses of people would die unnecessarily.

This dismal prophecy theoretically could be averted by individual moral restraints that repress an otherwise "strong inclination" to produce children promiscuously. Malthus observed, however, that individual moral restraint was an insufficient force because it was weakened by a "general corruption of morals, with regard to sex." Since promiscuous morality prevailed among some groups, the only way to limit the population was to allow those individuals who engaged in improvident "excesses to be subject to any cause, whether arising from vice or misery, which in any degree contributes to shorten the natural duration of human life." As if a modern Book of Job, these causes are specified to include: "all unwholesome occupations, severe labor and exposure to the seasons, extreme poverty, bad nursing of children . . . the whole train of common diseases and epidemics, wars, plague and famine" (Malthus 1967, 13–14). Universal natural forces would establish the balance between food and population. Intervention by government was unnecessary, even counterproductive.

Malthus's notion of economic development subjected "lower

classes of society to distress," thereby preventing substantially improved conditions. The cycle would be ameliorated by lower wages and harder work. He stated that "the laborer therefore must do more work to earn the same as he did before" (Malthus 1967, 15). Increased industriousness, combined with large amounts of cheap labor, would spur landowners and capitalists to hire more labor and thereby produce more goods, which, in time, would bring the laboring class back to the subsistence level. But this hopeful cycle, too, would run its course. As the conditions of life for the improvident mass of humanity become more comfortable, the population begins to outstrip food supplies. In Malthus's mind, this oscillation is inexorable. Malthus argued that remedial legislation was human interference with "nature's laws" and could not improve the condition of the poor because it would create more misery than it alleviated. Not only were the poor morally responsible for their own misery through excessive birth rates, but also they would continue to propagate and thus create a greater imbalance in the food-population equation if they were aided by unnatural forces, such as charity or "poor law" legislation. Poverty was testimony to the lower classes' outrageous violation of natural law. Although it had no basis in fact, Malthus's dour philosophy was seized upon by aristocratic and middle-class circles because it refuted radical explanations of social ills. It was a philosophic and economic defense the status quo could use against challenges to its rule.

The Eugenics Movement

Across the Atlantic, social conditions were different and worries about an overpopulating lower class seemed out of place. There was no landed aristocracy, the land area was much larger, the working class was not yet seen as a viable threat, industrialization came later and at a much accelerated pace, and the need for an expanding labor force was a more significant problem. In contrast to England, resources were abundant and employers were more concerned with the problem of labor shortages. Although indentured servants and convicts were invaluable in supplying needed labor in the early development of America, the most effective remedy for labor shortage came from Africa; ships hauled cargos of blacks to work the fields of the South. From 1830 to 1930 millions of Europeans made the long and arduous journey to the United States. Before 1880, while immigration was still uncontrolled, approximately ten million Europeans came to the United States, chiefly from northern and western Europe; U.S. society at that time was rural and agrarian. After 1880, coinciding with America's transition to a commercial and industrial power and a more urban society, there was a sharp and steady rise of immigrants from eastern and southern Europe. Slavs, Jews, Italians, Poles, Russians, and others came to America, and "quality" of population became the dominant issue. Population control had a strong eugenic component in America, at least until the experience of Hitler's Germany.

Eugenics is a branch of the study of human heredity, applying genetic principles to the "improvement" of the human race. It has followed two general directions: (1) positive eugenics, which concentrates on means to increase the "breeding" opportunities of especially "fit" individuals (e.g., large families for the wealthy and sperm banks for Nobel Laureates), and (2) negative eugenics, which emphasizes restrictions both on breeding for particularly "unfit" types and on immigration from certain countries. Eugenicists of the late 1800s and early 1900s possessed a racial as well as a class bias: Anglo-Saxon or "Nordic" types were the "fittest." Within the white race a three-tiered hierarchy existed: Nordic (Protestant, Northern Europe), Alpine (Catholic, Central and Eastern Europe), and Mediterranean (Catholic, Southern Europe).

Joseph de Gobineau (1816–1882) fabricated a theory about the inherent inequality among human races, which placed the Teutonic, or German, race at the apex and generally ranked races according to whiteness of skin. He offered a scientific explanation of why the lower races could never achieve higher levels of civilization. Europeans cited his views to justify the human costs of imperialism in Africa and Asia. Even before Gobineau's *Inequality of Races* was translated into English in 1915, Americans cited him in defense of slavery in the South (Chase 1977).

Henry Cabot Lodge and other young, mostly Harvard-educated, Boston Brahamins found Gobineau's racial theory very appealing in the 1870s. For them, the great Anglo-Saxon-Teutonic blood that had made North America great was being diluted by Irish and Italian immigrants. One remedy, to restrict immigration, put forth by the Immigration Restriction League, founded in 1894, was given a large boost when Senator Henry Cabot Lodge proposed a literacy test for immigrants. The test was proposed as an anti-immigration weapon in much the same way that literacy and property tests and poll taxes were introduced to legally disenfranchise newly emancipated blacks in the South in the 1880s and 1890s. Lodge's anti-immigration bill passed, but was vetoed by President Cleveland in 1897.

There was a strain between the industrialists' need for a large, cheap supply of labor and the elite's desire to restrict immigration. This strain within elite circles blocked the emergence of a consensus on immigration policy and restrained the eugenicists' popularity as long as a large supply of cheap labor was needed and the American working class posed little political threat. Nonetheless, the eugenics movement spread from its base in Boston to the whole nation and to wider segments of the population.

Eugenics can be conceptualized as an ideology that was nurtured by prosperous, Anglo-Saxon, Protestant Americans. It offered a robust view of society that would protect their status, prestige, privilege, and property. This view blamed the victims for the social problems associated with an industrial society, scientifically affixed class structure with heredity, and proposed solutions for many societal ills. While the eugenic movement was nurtured by and served the interests of wealthy, white Anglo-Saxon Protestants (WASPs), it periodically gained popular support. It can also be seen as a countermovement that enthralled sections of the American working class with appeals to racial and ethnic superiority.

In the United States, the patron saint of the eugenics movement was Charles Davenport, Harvard-educated, who was a tireless worker for various genetic and eugenic causes from 1900 to 1935. In 1904 he persuaded the Carnegie Foundation to establish a laboratory for experimental evolution. In 1907 he prevailed upon Mrs. E. H. (Mary) Harriman to contribute to the founding of the Eugenics Record Office. From these two institutions, Davenport and the eugenics movement acquired scientific respectability and generated political support for their theories of human heredity and social evolution.

The First International Eugenics Congress was held in London in 1912. Besides Davenport, other prominent Americans participated: Alexander Graham Bell; Charles Eliot, president emeritus of Harvard; and David Starr-Jordon, president of Stanford. One section of the Congress was devoted to papers on "Consideration of the practical applications of Eugenic Principles." One such practical application called for "prevention of the propagation of the Unfit by segregation and sterilization" (First International Eugenics Congress 1912).

So that there be no mistake about the intentions of the eugenic movement, Harry H. Laughlin of the Eugenics Record Office drafted a model sterilization law for eugenic adherents to present to their state legislatures. This model law defined "a socially inadequate person" as someone who "fails chronically," among other things, "as a useful member of the organized social life of the state." "Socially inadequate classes" included the feeble-minded, the delinquent and wayward, epileptics, the blind or deaf, deformed, and the "dependent (including orphans, ne'er-do-wells, the homeless, tramps and paupers)." A state eugenics agent was empowered to investigate a person's heredity, to make arrests, and to cause the offender to be sterilized (Laughlin 1930, 65).

In the United States the first eugenic law was passed in Indiana in 1907; twenty-nine others would follow. According to a leading expert, these laws resulted from the persuasion of a few influential individuals, not popular sentiment in their favor (Ludmerer 1972). One leading proponent of compulsory sterilization conceded that the "laws enacted have usually been put there by some very small energetic group of enthusiasts, who have influence in their legislature." He lamented that "this movement for race betterment is, as yet, little more than the hobby of a few groups of people, and does not really indicate the adoption of settled policy" (Ludmerer 1972, 94–95). The origins of California's 1909 eugenic law provides a case in point. C. M. Goethe, a businessman, takes credit:

> The Human Sterilization Movement had at least one beginning in my office back in the days of Dr. Hatch. He was then Secretary of the State Board of Health. In his private practice, he had specialized in mental diseases. He was convinced that certain tendencies thereto were inherited. He and I worked out the first sterilization law. Frankly, we slipped it through the California Legislature before the groups that we knew would fight it, grasped what had been done. The strategy then was to proceed under the law and accumulate a sufficient volume of case material [Goethe 1945a].

After the California law was passed, Eugene Gosney, an attorney and a stock breeder, became enthusiastically acquainted with eugenics. He formed the Human Betterment Foundation. In a 1945 letter, written thirty-six years after the law was passed, Goethe wrote that the Human Betterment Foundation would be well endowed by Gosney, who "believed his grants would make a perpetual $5,000,000 endowment. It is a tragedy that this has shrunk to about $200,000" (Goethe 1945b).

By 1931 thirty states had eugenics laws. While not massively enforced—twenty thousand sterilizations by 1935—the laws codified a eugenicist's conception of social relations as well as enacting a restrictive population-control solution. The symbolic value of the law is important. Eugenicists advocated state control as a means to achieve their goals.

To understand the eugenicists' fervor, one must realize that they were influenced by the social and intellectual climate of an era dominated by social Darwinism and Herbert Spencer. One powerful component was the social Darwinist fear that the quality of American stock was deteriorating. Institutions of charity, education, welfare, and medicine, which enabled the less "fit" to survive, were suspect because they interfered with natural selection (Hofstadter 1959; Schwendinger and Schwendinger 1974). This apprehension was accentuated by the widely held belief of a "differential birth rate"—the less fit procreated more than the fit (Ludmerer 1972; Popenoe and Williams 1934). Patrician families of New England perceived this threat, and they were the most active in responding to it.

Perhaps the greatest triumph of the eugenics movement was the passage of the Johnson Act in 1924. Supported by both big business interests and organized labor, the passage of this law severely restricted the quota of new immigrants from Eastern Europe and Mediterranean countries. Craft labor wanted to protect jobs and wages; sections of business wanted protection from foreign, radical influences; and the eugenicists wished to exclude Alpine and Mediterranean types (Higham 1965; Ludmerer 1972). Social problems associated with an ascendant, industrializing economy, such as urban social disorganization, periodic unemployment, and labor agitation, were conveniently defined as being "eugenic" in origin. It was in this period that eugenic doctrines were brought most forcibly into the arena of public opinion and had the greatest impact. The House Committee on Immigration and Naturalization appointed an "expert eugenics agent" in 1920. This expert, Harry Laughlin, the author of the model sterilization laws, presented the unchallenged view that the new wave of biologically inferior immigrants, typically non-Wasp, and from Southern and Eastern Europe, threatened to wipe out the native stock. In 1922 testimony, "Analysis of America's Modern Melting Pot," Congress's expert eugenics agent presented his findings. "Making all logical allowances for environmental conditions," he testified, "the recent immigrants, as a whole, present a higher percentage of inborn socially inadequate qualities than do the older stocks" (Ludmerer 1972, 101).

After 1924 scientific geneticists began to distinguish themselves from the eugenicists, and openly criticized the eugenics movement for the overt racist propaganda it published in the name of science. But the damage had already been done, and its undoing could never be accomplished entirely. Immigration from eastern and southern European countries was severely restricted by laws that were not repealed until 1965.

Eugenicists and their supporters overwhelmingly came from white, Anglo-Saxon, Protestant, patrician families. They were educators, scientists, clergymen, professors, and doctors (Ludmerer

1972, 16). The financiers of the movement included some of the
most well-known businessmen, investors, bankers, and philanthropists of the era. Considerable financial support for the eugenics
movement came from people like Corcoran Tom, vice-president of
the American Security and Trust Company; Mrs. E. H. (Mary)
Harriman; J. H. Kellogg, founder of Kellogg Foods; Robert D.
Ward, a member of the Saltonstall family of Boston; Madison Grant,
New York lawyer from a patrician family; C. M. Goethe, California
businessman; Eugene Gosney, a wealthy California attorney, stock
breeder, and founder of the Human Betterment Foundation; members
of the Carnegie Foundation; and Henry F. Osborn, paleontologist
from an upper-class family. Eugenics attracted these supporters for a
variety of reasons. They tacitly identified "fit" with the upper classes
and "unfit" with the lower classes. From their perspective the quality
of America's population was endangered by hordes of immigrants.
Ethnocentrism, a fear of status revolution, and a concrete political
threat from America's working class provided fertile terrain for the
growth of the eugenics movement throughout the first quarter of the
twentieth century.

   Rising numbers of immigrants threatened the power and prestige
of the propertied class and patrician Americans. There were many
attempts to preserve dominant social relations: the Prohibition movement, the rise of "society" and the Social Register to exclude those
of ill breeding, and the Johnson Act. In the 1910s, immigrants were
associated with the increasing radicalization of workers in general,
and the Industrial Workers of the World in particular. Suspicion of
immigrants and foreigners was heightened during World War I. After
the war immigrants were associated with the Palmer Raids of 1919
and the Red Scare of the 1920s. The eugenics movement lent a scientific grounding for antilabor views. By focusing on both class and
racial challenges, the propertied class simultaneously united on the
basis of class consolidation and segmented the working class along
race and ethnic lines. A eugenic view of race and national origin carried a strong emotional appeal not only to elites, but also to many
Americans. The movement had nurtured attitudes of racism, superiority, and outright hatred among the American people—all in the
name of science.

Eugenicists not only spoke about biological human heredity, but also had ready explanations about the origin of America's class structure. William McDougall, a prominent Harvard psychology professor, proclaimed that "the economic stratification of society corresponds in some degree with the distribution through the population of the more desirable human qualities, more especially the quality of intelligence" (McDougall 1923, 373).

Despite its fundamental racism, the eugenics movement appeared as a "reform" because it emerged at a time when most Americans liked to think of themselves as reformers. Social reformers and progressives were also attracted to the eugenics movement. E. A. Ross, the controversial Wisconsin sociologist and progressive, was an articulate spokesman for state intervention as a means to achieve eugenic goals. Like the progressive movement, eugenics accepted the principle of state action toward a common end (Hofstadter 1959). Philosophically, these movements shared views of race based on social Darwinism. They parted company, however, on issues of domestic social reform such as sanitation laws, labor laws, and consumer protection.

Eugenics held out the enticing possibility of social control through principles of biological efficiency. It appealed to progressives concerned about adjusting American life and institutions to the facts of modern industrialism. Eugenics held out the possibility that society could limit family size among the poor, improve maternal and child health, weed out the physically and mentally unfit, and control the size of selected populations. Some stated these goals in the utopian terms of social revolution. The eugenicists' belief in bettering society through a "scientific" method of biological engineering thus carried a strong appeal to social reformers, but the message was heavily weighted with notions of elitism and racism. The early birth control and women's movements also agreed with part of the eugenicist's conception.

Eugenic ideas, nurtured and developed by elites, found broad acceptance among feminists, progressives, socialists, and, gradually, the working class and the poor. This acceptance occurred partly because the eugenics movement openly articulated the notion that one should not have more children than one can care for. It is an idea that can be supported by reformers or revolutionaries from any political perspective, yet it became widely internalized in popular culture in a Malthusian manner.

Pseudosciences like eugenics must be understood as a social phenomenon. When the ratio of data to social impact is low, as Stephen Gould points out, "scientific attitudes may be little more than an oblique record of social change" (Gould 1981, 22). The social prejudices of the eugenics science resulted mostly from a priori convictions about society. The unconscious biases record subtle and inescapable constraints of culture and class. The biases, for most, were unknowingly influential, and most scientists believed they were pursuing the unsullied truth. For others, though, like Madison Grant and Harry Laughlin, who scribbled on a 1934 newspaper article that "Hitler should be made an honorary member of the ERA [Eugenics Record Association]," the bias was intentional, vicious, and dogmatic (Hirsch 1984). Genuine advances in genetics had great difficulty overcoming these entrenched social attitudes. Germany enacted a sterilization law in 1933 that ordered the sterilization of "undesirable" groups suspected of polluting the purity of German blood. This was done through decrees, "race bureaus," courts, and even judges—all to the admiring approval of leaders of the American eugenics movement like Harry Laughlin, Lathrop Stoddard, and Frederick Osborn. Mere scientific validity, rarely, if ever, suffices to undo the consequences of ideologies like eugenics. The death knell for the eugenics movement was sounded more from Hitler's horrors than from its atrophying, pseudoscientific origins.

Early Feminists and Margaret Sanger (1883–1966)

The women's movement made the first explicit demand for birth control in the 1840s. The movement, called *Voluntary Motherhood,* maintained that willing mothers would be better mothers. Reflecting Victorian era morality, voluntary-motherhood advocates focused on controlling male sexuality rather than simply preventing unwanted pregnancies. Thus these early feminists were opposed to the legalization of birth control, advocating instead either periodic or

long-term abstinence (Gordon 1981). Voluntary-motherhood advocates were part of a larger women's rights-movement that was concerned about suffrage, revisions of property rights, and better job opportunities. Linda Gordon argues that the essence of this phase of
feminism was an "anger at the suppression of the capabilities and
aspirations of women as individuals" (Gordon 1981, 81). Gordon
sees the Comstock Law of 1873 as an antifeminist backlash. This law
made it a crime to send obscene material through the mail and listed
birth control as an obscene subject.

Abortion became a remarkably widespread practice between 1840
and 1880. Historian James Mohr writes that, along with a sharp rise
in incidence, abortion became publicly visible (Mohr 1978). Furthermore, the social character of the practice changed. Increasingly, Mohr
argues, those seeking abortion "appeared to be married, native-born,
Protestant women, frequently of middle- or upper-class status"
(Mohr 1978, 86), not young women trying to hide illegitimacy or
infidelity from a disapproving family or society. During this period,
many believed that a reduction in family size reflected an increased
autonomy for women within the traditional family framework.

Public acceptance toward abortion changed as a result of the successful efforts of physicians to establish a professional monopoly
over medical services. In order to put their "quack" rivals—midwives and herbalists—out of business, doctors found it convenient to
launch a campaign against abortion. Between 1860 and 1890 every
state enacted laws stipulating that abortion could be performed only
by physicians and only when a mother's life was in danger; thus, a
period of considerable tolerance toward abortion in the United States
ended. The federal government contributed to this effort by passing
the Comstock Law, which did not move against the practice of abortion, but against the "obscene" character of abortion ads (Mohr
1978). The anti-abortion and anti-feminist backlash thus had intermingling overtones.

In the early twentieth century, another group of feminists had
different ideas about contraception. The birth-control movement
started in the company of anarchists, socialists, and feminists. Emma
Goldman was jailed for speaking on birth control, and the young

Margaret Sanger advocated it in her independent, feminist journal, *The Woman Rebel*, which was founded in 1914. At first the movement did not attract support from the middle class, who saw birth control as a wicked scheme to "take penalty out of vice" (cited in Ehrenreich and English 1973, 68).

The majority of American socialists believed that birth control was a dangerous distraction from class struggle. While some were active in the birth-control movement, most were swayed by the old anti-Malthusian argument. In America, as in Europe, birth control was caught up in the ancient battle of Marx versus Malthus (Rowbotham 1974). The cause of birth control was hampered because orthodox socialists equated birth control with neo-Malthusianism. Many male progressives saw birth control as threatening in both political and personal terms. For most in this time period, birth control became intertwined with population control and hence the two ideas were no longer separable.

As the birth-control movement matured under Margaret Sanger's leadership, it repudiated its radical origins and support and began to seek respectable, middle-class support instead. In the process, it made a frank appeal to middle-class interests and concerns. Sanger, socialist and heroine of feminist agitation during this period, spent her life campaigning for birth control, arguing that no woman is free unless she controls her body and can choose consciously whether she will or will not be a mother and how many children she will have. This struck a responsive chord among middle- and upper-class women because the eugenics movement was telling them it was their duty to have large families. The positive eugenic solution of "fit" individuals having large families placed an oppressive burden on women. By 1919 she was giving her former socialist views a new twist, "All our problems are the result of overbreeding among the working class" (cited in Kennedy 1970, 112). By 1922 she had repudiated her earlier radicalism. She now supported the Malthusian ideas she had once so strenuously fought: misery was attributable not to economics and political dislocation, but to the fecundity of the working class itself.

Sanger was also lured by other aspects of the eugenics argument. "More children from the fit, less from the unfit—that is the chief issue of birth control," she wrote in 1919 (cited in Kennedy, 1970, 115). She complained that although the racial quotas of the Johnson Act of 1924 had already

> . . . taken steps to control the quality of population . . . we close our gates to the so-called undesirables from other countries, we make no attempt to cut down the rapid multiplication of the unfit and undesirables at home. . . . When we view the political situation aɴd realize that a moron's vote is as good as an intelligent, educated and thinking citizen, we may well pause and ask ourselves, Is America safe for democracy?

The United States should "set a sensible example to the world by offering a bonus or yearly pension to all obvious unfit parents to allow themselves to be sterilized" (Sanger 1926, 299). Her biographer, David Kennedy, says that Sanger "had first embraced eugenic rhetoric as just another addition to her grab-bag of arguments for contraception." But eugenic arguments soon dominated and "underscored the conversion of the birth-control movement from a radical program of social disruption to a conservative program of social control" (Kennedy 1970, 121).

One reason for this conversion is that Sanger despaired of any meaningful support coming from radicals or the "wives of the wage slaves," as she called them, so instead she turned "to the women of wealth and intelligence" for help (Drinnon 1961, 170). With considerable ability she guided the birth-control movement into respectable channels by emphasizing the need for legislation that would give doctors—and only doctors—the right to impart contraceptive information. Sanger began to resent Goldman and other radicals and socialists who refused to consider birth control a panacea. Some feminist birth control advocates like Mary Ware Dennett criticized Sanger's strategy, arguing that accepting male medical control of contraception was contradictory to the principle of woman's control over her own fertility. Others, like revolutionary socialist Antoinette Konikow, argued that allowing doctors to take charge transformed a popular women's rights issue into a narrow medical model, which depoliticizes issues of concern to women.

The movement to win acceptance and legality for birth control was shaped by its changing sources of support, internal politics, response to opposition, and Sanger's charismatic leadership. The accommodation and settling of intramural rivalries occurred in 1942 with the formation of the Planned Parenthood Federation of America, which prompted desperately needed reforms and consolidated concrete gains for women's aspirations. The price of the gains was considerable. This new businesslike organization pioneered a family-planning model that stressed professional medical supervision and planning in determining the conditions of fertility control, virtually excluding the women's rights issues that gave rise to the movement. Rosalind Petchesky argues that the professionalization of birth control, besides perverting its feminist aspects, "involves the desexualization of the birth control issue" (Petchesky 1984, 93). By this she means that a "hygienic" concept of sex as strictly marital, monogamous, heterosexual, and a "good adjustment" to marriage was stressed. A "medicalized" notion of fertility control was supposed to decontaminate and depoliticize the issue, suppressing the issues of sexuality and woman's sexual nature altogether. One of the ironies in the transition from a feminist birth-control movement to a professionalized, hygienic, family planning notion is that the movement to "free women from the fetters of male tyranny" deliberately called upon a male doctor to be the first head of Planned Parenthood (Kennedy 1970, 270).

Black radicals in the early twentieth century supported birth control because they saw it as a tool for the self-determination of black Americans. In the 1920s, however, with the rising influence of the eugenicists and, later, the population controllers, blacks became wary of birth control programs. Angela Davis writes that the birth-control movement of the 1930s capitulated to "the racism associated with eugenic ideas." Birth control "had been robbed of its progressive potential, advocating for people of color not the individual right to *birth control*, but rather the racist strategy of *population control*" (Davis 1981, 215). In 1973 black Congresswomen Shirley Chisholm, Barbara Jordan, Yvonne Burke, and Cardiss Collins wrote Caspar Weinberger, secretary of Health, Education, and Welfare, warning that cases of sterilization abuse "raised doubts in the minds of minority citizens concerning the voluntary nature of federally funded family planning programs" (U.S. Senate Subcommittee on Health 1973, 1562–63). Faced with harsh material realities and having to struggle arduously with many sacrifices to achieve even the mildest reform, blacks have a deep-rooted suspicion about the motives of programs that virtually give away birth-control services to minorities. There is abundant historical evidence to support this suspicion.

A New Ideological Basis for Population Control

For Malthusian ideas to survive the discredited eugenics movement they would have to conform to the social realities of the 1930s. Prior to the 1930s, although immigrants were disliked, labor was needed. With the onset of massive unemployment and fear of organized labor, the focus of concern shifted. While race and ethnic origins would remain important, class concerns came to the fore as a basis of continued population control. Shorn of its scientific trappings in the late 1920s, when some geneticists denounced the eugenics movement, and reflecting the new realities and problems of the Depression, population control would come to rest on new social footing.

Historical evidence shows continuous development in population-control thinking from the early 1920s to World War II, and beyond. A continuous development implies a reorientation in tactics, not in underlying social views or political goals. This can be traced both ideologically and organizationally by examining the contributions of Frederick Osborn, Clarence J. Gamble, and the Association for Voluntary Sterilization (AVS). Notably, the impact of these men and the organizations with which they associated can be measured not only by specific accomplishments, but also by the modification (for preservation) of population-control objectives.

Frederick Osborn (1889–1981)

The American Eugenics Society (AES) was founded in 1921 at the Second International Conference on Eugenics in New York. The society was located in New Haven, Connecticut, until the early

1950s, when the Population Council in New York offered space and financial assistance. Nearly all important eugenicists between 1921 and the 1950s belonged to the AES; their primary goals were educational, thus they sponsored exhibitions at country fairs and contests for the best essays and sermons on eugenics. The AES was the most important vehicle for eugenics education in America (Ludmerer 1972).

Frederick Osborn, secretary of the society from 1928 to 1972, dedicated most of his life to the eugenics movement and was a major figure in shaping society policy. He retired early from his positions as bank president and railroad executive to study genetics, psychology, and sociology. Dissatisfied with what he thought were the extreme prejudices of the eugenics movement, he used his influence to replace the flagrant racists with people of scientific reputation and more "balanced views" (Allen and Mehler 1977; Ludmerer 1972). According to one historian, Osborn forged a new leadership, which was "generally interested in mankind's genetic future" and which "rejected the class and race biases of their predecessors" and even "admitted the foolishness of earlier eugenicists' pronouncements." This new leadership "propounded a new eugenic creed which was scientifically and philosophically attuned to a changed America" (Ludmerer 1972, 174).

But the tactics and tone appear to have changed much more than the underlying goals. Allen and Mehler (1977, 12–13) cited a circular letter of 1937, in which Osborn summarized the proceeding of an AES conference on eugenics:

> A brief history of the origin and development of eugenic sterilization showed the originality of the United States where all the first laws were initiated, and indicated the lack of thoroughness of our people in their failure to follow through.
>
> In Germany, the need for eugenic measures was not only the result of the war [World War I], but also of the increasing urbanization and mobilization of her people, resulting in the location of families in new surroundings where they were not known by their neighbors or by the authorities, which presented serious problems.
>
> Changes in both increasing urbanization and mobility of her people are rapidly taking place in the United States also.

The German sterilization program is apparently an excellent one, although it is generally doubted whether equal or better results might not have been obtained by a voluntary rather than a compulsory system.

Taken altogether, recent developments in Germany constitute perhaps the most important experiment which has ever been tried.

While Osborn believed himself to be a moderate man of balanced views who drastically altered the course of eugenics to create a "new" scientific eugenics, it is clear that he maintained the basic aims of the older eugenicists. Like them, he believed in the inherent inferiority of women: "the present emphasis on intellectual achievement may be a great handicap to women trying to develop their natural feminine roles" (cited in Allen and Mehler 1977, 13). According to Allen and Mehler, Osborn also appears to have accepted the belief that America's class structure was a product of natural evolution. He thought these assumptions to be scientific. Developments in genetics and the Nazis' use of sterilization dampened popular enthusiasm for the eugenics movement in the United States. Despite this denouement, eugenic ideas continued to ebb and flow with the times as an important factor in birth control history. Osborn and the AES kept the ideas alive. He would also make significant contributions later while serving as trustee of the Population Council from 1952 until 1968, and as its president from 1957 to 1959.

Clarence J. Gamble (1894–1966)

The social and ideological foundation for population control adapted to the changed social circumstances of the Depression. It would alter again after World War II. This critical bridge to the current era saw the social-construction of new population-control themes for America. One person who bridged this transition was Clarence J. Gamble. Doctor, scientist, influential advocate of birth control and population control, and Ivory soap heir, Gamble tried to personally orchestrate the birth- and population-control movements from the late 1920s until his death in 1966. For him, the two movements were synonymous. He devoted a large part of his share of the Proctor and

Gamble fortune, energy, and intelligence to a search for better contraception. He either personally participated, initiated, organized, or
helped to finance virtually every experiment in population control
during this period. At one time or another, he was a member of just
about every important organization in the field, heading many of
them for short periods of time. Gamble started the Pathfinder Fund,
which carries out his legacy today (Reed 1978). He had few peers
who knew less about or financed more projects on human fertility.

Born in 1894, he carried on the family's belief in Christian
stewardship. At twenty-one he inherited his first million dollars, on
the condition that he contribute at least one-tenth of his income to
good causes. The estate had grown to about $50 million at the time
of his death. Like his brothers, Clarence was educated at Princeton.
He graduated, second in his class, from Harvard Medical School in
1920 and won a coveted internship at Massachusetts General Hospital. But he wanted to be a researcher, and his wealth gave him a
unique opportunity to define his research interests. After an un-
distinguished research apprenticeship at the University of Pennsylvania, Gamble's life work began in earnest.

His activities in the birth-control movement began in 1929, during a period of declining birth rates and economic depression. For
him, birth control was a reform that went beyond the palliatives of
the New Deal. Birth control struck at what Gamble, and many other
of its wealthy patrons, saw as a fundamental source of social disorder: differential fertility between classes. "His mission," in the
words of a sympathetic biographer, "was to make the world safe for
his kind of people, the frugal, hard-working, and prosperous leaders
of American society" (Reed 1978, 227).

Friends of Gamble started a birth-control clinic in Philadelphia
under the auspices of the Committee for Maternal Health Betterment. Gamble's involvement with the clinic began when he was
asked to determine which contraceptive jellies were most effective.
From then on Gamble searched for a fertility-control method that
was the simplest, most effective, and least dependent on doctors.
Gamble wanted to find a new method of fertility control that would
be affordable for the poor and would skirt the professional monopoly

of doctors. By 1933 nine clinics were operating in Pennsylvania, supported by a small group of philanthropists including Gamble. Although birth-control clinics for the poor were greatly needed, they had to be privately funded because the Depression was rapidly exhausting the resources of community charity. Public assistance was forbidden; even relaying birth-control information across state lines was a federal crime.

As a physician and scientist with much free time and a strong sense of mission, Gamble took up his calling. In the fall of 1933 he was elected president of the Pennsylvania Birth Control Federation. Under his leadership the organization's literature clearly and consistently stressed a denunciation of New Deal welfare coupled with a plea for privately funded birth control. Making birth control available for the swelling ranks of the poor might render welfare less of a burden. Birth control was pitched as one way to lessen the impact of the Depression—the poor could have fewer hungry children and the wealthy would not have to support them. One 1935 fund-raising letter asserted that the birth rate of the unemployed was 60 percent higher than among the employed. The solicitation for money for the Pennsylvania Birth Control Federation claimed "that each dollar will multiply itself by hundreds in lessening the load of debt that the next generation must pay. Our children will have to care for those who are now being born and raised in the crippling atmosphere of public relief" (Gamble 1935).

Another of the federation's pamphlets warned that the "New Relief" had transformed private, charitable case work into mass public welfare. Rehabilitation was no longer stressed; in its place was an acceptance of the unending need to support millions of people. There was imminent danger of a permanent and growing class of social parasites. "With our relief and other social welfare expenditures as high as they are, is it not time that the program of sterilization of the unfit be considered anew," the pamphlet asked rhetorically, then answered that "gigantic expenditures for the new relief ought to interest us in any sane and constructive proposal which will look toward the lightening of our social welfare load in any of its phases." The philosophical and practical appeal is succinct: "to carry on relief

. . . and to fail to provide them with every opportunity and facility which will permit them sanely to control their reproduction in the light of their present circumstances, is both bad business and bad social statesmanship." Then, in a wider appeal for support, and one that may sound familiar today, "If there is one right which every family should have, it is that of self-determination in the function of bringing new life into the world; for self-respecting families struggling under the economic distress, that right and its exercise becomes doubly important" (Bossard 1934, 5,7).

Under Gamble's stewardship the Pennsylvania Birth Control Federation reasoned that giving money to birth-control clinics to prevent the production of relief babies was wiser than caring for them once they were born. Birth control provided a means for going beyond mere amelioration, a positive step toward reducing the numbers of the indigent. A leaflet addressed to "Mr. and Mrs. Taxpayer" crassly asked: "How many children would you add to your family if you were absolutely dependent upon public relief? The remedy—contraceptive advice . . ." (Pennsylvania Birth Control Federation 1934). Another piece of literature argued that "birth control prevents destitution and dependency. It gives relief to the overburdened taxpayer by preventing the births of children who can only be cared for at public expense." In 1934, 64,000 babies were born to families on relief in Pennsylvania. The children's first year cost the taxpayers roughly $10 million, an expense that, according to the Pennsylvania Birth Control Federation, could have been spared for ten dollars' worth of birth-control advice. These babies, "who could hardly be said to have been wanted by anyone, would not have been born" (Pennsylvania Birth Control Federation 1936). In a letter to "Uncle Ray," thanking him for a $150 donation, Gamble estimated "that your contribution is saving Philadelphia charities some $60,000" (Gamble 1933).

The literature distributed under Gamble's stewardship reveals overt themes of population control. Charitable investments in birth control were intended to pay population-control dividends in the form of tax relief. While literature proposed a social ethic on the right of every child to be wanted, it ignored the possibility that those on relief might want children, or that they might be religiously opposed to contraception. It presumed that a dependent on relief had no right to have a child. Society, in its self-defense, could demand the right to control fertility. Gamble believed that differential fertility among classes posed a serious threat to the future of civilization. He had five children, but this did not conflict with his crusade for birth control because "good stock" who could take care of their own should have more children (Reed 1978).

Gamble was ambivalent about the merits of a college education for women. He reasoned that educated women, knowledgeable about birth control, had fewer children; these smart, well-to-do women were, however, the ones who should practice positive eugenics and have more children. He sponsored a stork derby at Bryn Mawr College for the class having the highest birth rate in the first ten years after graduation (Williams and Williams 1978). Ironically, it is here that Gamble's ideas come closest to what social scientists know about fertility behavior. The better educated the woman, the more likely she is to work for satisfaction—and the less likely she is to have a large family. If education generally correlates with childbearing, one could turn Gamble's logic on its head and propose a college education for all women to lower the birthrate. But contemplating a college education for poor women cuts across the grain of the underlying eugenic and population-control assumptions.

Gamble's influence on the Pennsylvania Birth Control Federation was just one example of his involvement in a crusade to bring population control to poor people. He tested contraceptive jellies; financed population-control experiments in Logan County, West Virginia; and helped to initiate, organize, and finance the institutional support system that facilitated Puerto Rico's high rate of sterilization. His participation was widespread, and he significantly affected the course of family planning in America. At one time or another he was involved in the American Birth Control League, the National Committee on Maternal Health, the Association for Voluntary Sterilization, Planned Parenthood Federation, and the Worchester Foundation of Experimental Biology.

Clarence Gamble wanted to be known as a working philanthropist and not just as a rich man. He wanted his ideas and experiences to be treated seriously, on their own merits. His one inflexible requirement as a donor was that he be allowed to participate actively in the planning and execution of projects he sponsored; furthermore, he tried to manipulate existing organizations into sponsoring his pet programs. Gamble frequently peppered officials of birth control organizations with suggestions, requests, inquiries, and other meddling demands. Eventually, patience wore thin. One sanctioned biography says, "he never was an organizational man and never understood the dynamics of organizational process." As a result he was in constant conflict with officials of other organizations who complained that Gamble "nagged and pestered them to distraction" (Williams and Williams 1978, xiii). Frank Notestein, president of the Population Council, which was involved in a dispute with Gamble over patent and distribution rights to the Lippes loop intrauterine device, complained in 1965 that Gamble was "flying like a bird over countries dropping loops" (Williams and Williams 1978, 358).

Gamble's efforts to promote contraceptive research were also hampered by conflict with professional organizations already established in the field. Power provided by money must be justified. Wealthy social activists often skirt this justification by channeling money into professional organizations. Gamble had less money than others, like John D. Rockefeller III, and he resented paying salaries to policy makers who, in his opinion, knew less about population than he (Reed 1978). Disagreements grew out of conflicting values. Gamble and Margaret Sanger worked together on many projects, including formation of the Birth Control Federation of America in 1939 and the International Planned Parenthood Federation; however, they disagreed on leadership styles and the autonomy of women.

Gamble's most ambitious, and arguably most successful, population-control experiment was in Puerto Rico. Because of pressure from Catholic officials in the United States, the Puerto Rican Emergency Relief Administration dropped its birth-control program in 1936, which was a re-election year for Roosevelt. Gamble dispatched a field worker to interview Dr. Ernest Gruening, administrator of the Puerto Rican Reconstruction Administration under Roosevelt. He later became Alaska's first senator. Gruening recommended that private clinics be organized to carry out the task of birth control (Gruening 1977; Williams and Williams 1978). Gamble sent field workers to the island to help organize these clinics and to rally public support by making it appear as if they had been initiated by Puerto Ricans. Birth-control services were desperately wanted by Puerto Rican women, but, seemingly, population-control programs featuring long-lasting, and sometimes experimental, drugs, devices, and procedures were delivered.

Gamble's field worker, Phyllis Page, set up the Maternal and Child Health Association, which was modeled on the constitution of a similar group she had set up in Berea, Kentucky (Williams and Williams 1978). Eventually a network of twenty-three privately sponsored clinics was organized. In 1937 the insular legislature passed a public health department-sponsored contraceptive program for the poor, which sanctioned birth-control advice and legalized sterilization, but not abortion. By 1939 contraceptive services were included in the Insular Health Department Program. Professional personnel and specially trained nurses were transferred from private clinics to the Health Department, whose services included experimental devices and procedures. Pharmaceutical companies, for instance, bid with one another to test their products in these clinics; donations were sought and received from them. Gamble provided funds so that Puerto Rican doctors could fly to New York to learn the latest sterilization techniques. Sterilization policy in the island's hospitals was described in a field worker's report to Gamble in 1946: "The policy of the hospital is to carry out sterilisations if the woman has three living children. In his [the acting director's] private practice two are enough." Furthermore, "It is the unofficial policy of the hospital not to admit (uncomplicated) multiparae if they do not submit to sterilisation" (Tietze 1946). Under such conditions, sterilizations are anything but voluntary.

The Puerto Rico experience teaches an important lesson about the politics of population and reproduction by showing how sterilization and abortion became artificially separated—one being outlawed, the other becoming the mainstay of policy. Rosalind Petchesky has observed that women's consciousness about birth-control possibilities was strongly influenced by the patriarchal authority of physicians, husbands and priests. In the context of traditional culture, "sterilization was less stigmatized and less offensive to the moral and patriarchal sensibilities of all three than any other form of contraception." In a Catholic culture largely antagonistic to birth control, sterilization is not as sinful as other methods of birth control, and "it can also be kept secret." (Petchesky 1981, 59). Sterilization, experienced by three generations of women, has become imbedded in the culture.

In Puerto Rico, as of 1968, abortions were virtually unavailable to the poor, but 35.3 percent of all women of reproductive age had been sterilized. One study reported that 36.1 percent of these women regret being sterilized and that three-quarters of them wanted more children and were unaware that the operation was irreversible (N.O.W.–New York 1978). Legal abortions are still virtually unobtainable; according to 1976 HEW data, 37.4 percent of childbearing-age women have been sterilized, financed by the Family Planning Association of Puerto Rico, which received 80 percent of its budget from HEW (Blair 1977). Puerto Rico has one of the highest rates of female sterilization found anywhere in the world. Gamble contributed greatly to translating desires for birth control into programs of population control.

The Association for Voluntary Sterilization

The Association for Voluntary Sterilization (AVS) is the most active organization advocating sterilization. The history of the organization reveals the changing basis—organizationally and ideologically—of population control, especially the role of sterilization. Founded in 1937 by an avowed eugenicist, Marian S. Olden, and seventeen other prominent New Jerseyites as the New Jersey League for Human Betterment, the initial focus was eugenic sterilization. The organization promoted a Sterilization Act for the State of New Jersey, lobbied for its passage, and tried to convince wardens and superintendents to sterilize inmates and patients. It changed its name in 1943 to Birthright, Inc., to indicate a national orientation. In 1950 it became the Association for Human Betterment; in 1962, the Human Betterment Association for Voluntary Sterilization; and in 1965, the Association for Voluntary Sterilization. When Olden founded the organization she was acting on her conviction that selective, eugenic sterilizations would solve social problems once and for all. A history of AVS says that "Olden was the Sterilization League of New Jersey and then Birthright" for the first eleven years of its existence (Vanessendelft 1978). The organization was identified with compulsory sterilization.

By World War II the emphasis on compulsory sterilization began to diminish, despite the dominance of eugenic ideas. Realizing that the public would not accept compulsory sterilization because of the Nazis' application, there was a gradual shift to voluntary sterilization. H. Curtis Wood, obstetrician and former president of Pennsylvania Planned Parenthood, was most responsible for the shift from compulsory to voluntary sterilization. He joined Birthright in 1943, becoming president two years later. One of his institutional goals was to incorporate sterilization and birthright into the larger Planned Parenthood organization (Vanessendelft 1978). There were frequent attempts to push Olden into the background because she was too parochial and unscientific, and her 'backward' views about compulsory, eugenic sterilization were a continuing source of embarrassment.

Wood's concerns were the reconstructed eugenic agenda for the 1940s: high fertility of poor families with low IQs, among the feeble-minded, the uneducated, and the poor, would lead to the collapse of American civilization. Unlike earlier coercive eugenicists, however, Wood emphasized the potentially persuasive role of doctors. He urged that socioeconomic reasons, along with eugenic ones, be treated as a "medical" indication for sterilization. He thought doctors were in a unique position to persuade patients to accept voluntary sterilization. The effect would be eugenic, even if patients' reasons were not; unlike birth control, permanent contraception would be achieved.

One reason for the shift to voluntary sterilization was an awareness that Birthright's goal of compulsory sterilization for the unfit had not succeeded. Organizations like Planned Parenthood persistently refused to include sterilization in their programs and to be anything but minimally cooperative. The eugenic sterilization movement was being isolated both from established birth control organizations and from the medical establishment. Wood's reorientation of tactics emphasizing professionals and doctors and ideology stressing voluntary sterilization succeeded ultimately in maintaining the viability of sterilization.

In 1943 Clarence J. Gamble joined Birthright, a fledgling organization that found his medical expertise and wealth attractive. Gamble sponsored field-work projects that had considerable autonomy from the rest of Birthright, and he was chairman of the field-work committee until 1947. In his first year, he raised $15,000, which gave him considerable influence over the projects and the organization, which raised only $4,355 in that year. Field work consisted of demonstration projects on sterilization. One project in Orange County, North Carolina tested school-age children to identify who should be considered for sterilization. Results indicated that 3 percent were either insane or "feebleminded" (Vanessendelft 1978). Other projects were aimed at convincing penal and health authorities of the benefits of eugenic sterilization. Eventually, Gamble's insistent meddling, hubris, and desire for control provoked internal strife, especially between Olden and him. Gamble's affiliation with Birthright was severed in 1947.

Olden, an avowed eugenicist, thought the Nazis had tarnished the image of eugenic sterilization. She attempted to salvage it. In the 1946 pamphlet "The ABC of Human Sterilization," published under the name of Birthright and reprinted in 1948, Olden wrote: "Was sterilization used by the Nazis as a punishment for racial 'crimes'? No. . . . Sterilization was restricted to special Health Courts staffed by medical personnel." And in a line that could hardly have been reassuring, she explained: "It was used to check the fertility of persons who were contributing to the biological deterioration of their people" (Olden 1946, 2). Olden was finally dismissed by the executive committee in 1948 so that the organization could be run by professionals and doctors.

Wood still believed in selective, compulsory sterilization, but he had little hope of achieving it in America; therefore, he emphasized voluntary sterilization for socioeconomic reasons (Vanessendelft 1978). The shift to voluntary sterilization was made immediately after World War II; yet how to gain respectability for AVS and how to convince social-welfare and birth-control agencies to make sterilization a part of their programs remained nagging problems.

In the 1950s, while the topic of birth-control methods was still publicly taboo, much private research and education were conducted. Wood and others in the Association for Human Betterment argued that sterilization was simply a form of birth control that was surer because it was permanent. Society could finally have an effective method of controlling fertility in the lower classes. This eugenic dream would be realized by technological advances that promised a safer, more effective, and cheaper procedure, even one that could be done on an outpatient or "band-aid" basis. But Wood, prone to impatience and impetuous comments, was not satisfied with a slow incremental approach; he wanted to educate obstetricians to perform postpartum sterilizations at their own discretion. He told a friend that he and fellow doctors had talked certain patients into sterilization on a strictly "voluntary" basis. "It is not hard to talk most of them into it during their pregnancies," he boasted. He insisted the task was "to educate the doctor to educate the patient. It seems too slow to try and educate the legislature" (cited in Vanessendelft 1978, 177).

As late as 1963 Wood thought sterilizations would reduce welfare abuse. He emphasized welfare costs that could be saved if sterilizations were practiced on the lower class. During the 1940s and 1950s socioeconomic reasons became increasingly important in the movement. The association set a high priority on voluntary sterilization for the poor and on encouraging professionals, particularly doctors, to promote it. In the 1960s, as the state's role in welfare programs increased and as sterilization became more acceptable, the association saw the use of tax dollars to promote and pay for sterilization as an increasingly important and logical progression.

Hugh Moore, the Dixie Cup king, ardent advocate of population control, and instigator of the Population Crisis Committee, infused the organization with money, professionalism, and a polished public-relations style. Moore took over the Human Betterment Association, became its president in 1964, changed its name to Association for Voluntary Sterilization, and raised enough money to hire a professional staff. When Moore died in 1972, AVS survived without his considerable help. In 1976 AVS received $1,696,000 from A.I.D. to set up sterilization programs overseas. Meanwhile, AVS literature continued to stress sterilization as a sound answer to the waste of "billions more of our tax dollars . . . on relief," and also to the "critical need to control population explosion" (Association for Voluntary Sterilization n.d., 6).

In the 1970s AVS continued to cite a laundry list of problems as reasons for encouraging voluntary sterilization. The indications for sterilization became all-encompassing, perhaps completing the circle back to Malthus. An AVS fund raising appeal asserted that "the population explosion, augmented by the birth of unwanted children to parents unable or unwilling to provide for them, is a basic cause of social ills in the United States." Further, "the catastrophic results of uncontrolled fertility are visible to us on all sides: slums, environmental pollution, and swelling relief rolls at home" (Association for Voluntary Sterilization n.d., 2).

Today, the AVS is considered to be the most respectable organization promoting sterilization. Their shifts—from compulsory to voluntary sterilization, from private to public financing, from a lay to a medical/professional organization, and from eugenic appeals to those of population explosion, welfare costs, and pollution—mirror the passage from one era to another. Eugenic and population-control motives remain intact; tactics and strategies have changed dramatically. Along the route from the all volunteer New Jersey League for Human Betterment in 1937 to the highly professional AVS of today, the organization has attracted and, in turn, been influenced by the leadership of Clarence J. Gamble, Hugh Moore, and others. Its patrons have included the wealthy and the "upper crust." Not nearly as influential as Planned Parenthood or the Population Council, AVS nonetheless has successfully helped to promote sterilization as a method of birth control and to make it acceptable to the public. Technological advances in sterilization techniques and the rooting of sterilization within the medical profession as a method of birth control cannot be disentangled from AVS's advocacy of it.

This selective history highlights several important points. One is that a Malthusian-inspired population-control movement has been present in America throughout the twentieth century. It gains popularity and flourishes in periods of economic difficulty and political retrenchment, and it also thrives as a countermovement feeding on existing cleavages in America's class, race, and ethnic composition. Another is that sterilization is only one tool of population control—immigration restriction and denial of services are other time-honored tools of the movement. While it is but one method, sterilization has held out the greatest promise as a permanent solution to the challenges and consequences of unwanted population growth. The brief glimpses of Malthus, the eugenics movement, Sanger, Osborn, Olden, Gamble, and AVS are intended to bring sterilization into clearer focus within the perspective of population control. In addition, this selective history reveals a thematic and organizational legacy that is crucial to understanding the current context of population control in the United States.

A population-control perspective has been developed and nurtured by specific groups of Americans. The ideas and money to give it expression historically emanates from wealthy Americans. From the Harriman-Kellogg-Carnegie-Osborn-Olden fascination with the eugenics movement to Gamble's single-minded pursuit of birth control for the poor to the Moore-Wood stewardship of the AVS, America's upper-class families have generously supported population control and eugenic sterilization; these views not only conformed to social life as they experienced it, but also served their own ends. Eugenic and population-control perspectives were not scientifically unchallenged in this period. Their popularity was due to organized social support, not scientific veracity or even efficacy. For example, the scientific support of the eugenics movement was being undermined by developments in genetics long before Hitler gave it a bad name in America. Despite this, some wealthy Anglo-Saxon Americans believed in and generously contributed to the eugenicists' scientifically invalid version of heredity. Franz Boas, an eminent anthropologist working on theories of evolution, attempted to raise funds for an African museum in the United States. Boas solicited many of the same funding sources as the eugenicists, but he was an anti-eugenicist who was developing a unique, nonlinear scale theory about racial evolution. His requests were denied, even though his ideas had scientific credibility.

One other example illustrates some of the consequences of ignoring scientific evidence in favor of a eugenics view of society. In 1912 a commission was established to determine the cause of pellagra. Dr. Joseph Goldberger, the Public Health Service's top field investigator, was assigned to the commission. Goldberger documented that pellagra was a disease caused by the inadequate diets of poor people, especially in the South, and his findings dominated the commission's first two reports. The prevention and cure of a disease that resulted in listlessness, mental illness, and even death were simple enough—provide wages that allowed the poor to purchase essential food: meats, poultry, fish, dairy products, and fresh fruits and vegetables. Goldberger thought the single crop economy of the South should be changed. He also believed that changing the diets of people in prisons, mental hospitals, and orphanages would prevent many deaths caused by pellagra.

Charles Davenport, director of the Eugenics Record Office, had become involved with the commission in 1913 and had published papers claiming that pellagra was hereditary. Rather than attributing mental illness and extreme lethargy among the poor to prevailing social conditions in the South, Davenport and the eugenicists ignored the evidence and persisted in seeing those conditions and pellagra as the natural and unchangeable products of heredity. Goldberger's discoveries made further research superfluous, so, in 1914, the two military doctors who headed the commission left for other assignments. Davenport stepped into this void, took control of the commission's work and guided the preparation of its third and final report in 1917, in which Goldberger's work, except for one footnote (Chase 1977), was ignored. The religious fervor of Charles Davenport, his pseudoscientific "facts," and the elite support system of the eugenics movement suppressed Goldberger's conclusions. From 1916 until 1933 the real causes, and prevention, of pellagra were ignored because they did not conform to a particular social view of the world. The price of ignorance was needless continued disease, lowered resistance to other diseases, mental illness, and the preventable deaths of at least fifty thousand people (Chase 1977).

Money provided the impetus and family names conferred the respectability, but the organizational social supports supplied the institutional legitimacy for the ideas. Organizations are usually perceived as detached from their benefactors, thus the specific interests of a small group can appear as universal concerns. University presidents, academics, social reformers, and writers helped popularize, sanitize, and lend credibility to the eugenic, population-control, and sterilization movements. Academics like Harvard's William McDougall, Wisconsin's E. A. Ross, and Paul Popenoe, along with social reformers like Margaret Sanger and popular writers like H. L. Mencken, employed their considerable, and often vitriolic, talents in the service of these movements. Despite the elitist bases of the ideas, they were usually cloaked in popular appeals directed at upper segments of the working class, whites, taxpayers, or environmentalists.

This social history also reveals the high price paid by the birth-control movement and Margaret Sanger to achieve sorely needed reforms. One significant cost was the changing basis on which this movement appealed for support: from poor and working women within a radical political context to middle- and upper-class women tied to eugenics and population-control support. This meant that birth control would be equated with racist and class-biased assumptions of who should reproduce. Another cost was the yielding of a fundamental tenet of feminism: birth control, a means for women to control their own reproductive capacity, became a mechanism of social control over the fertility of certain groups of women. The costs also included the continued suppression of abortion (Petchesky 1984).

Claims of ethnic, racial, and class superiority are the bedrock of population control. Generally, there has been a distinct shift from a

dominant ethnic and racial appeal to class appeals. This can be conceptualized as reflecting America's transition from a country needing
a labor force so desperately that quality, not quantity, was the major
problem. This shifted temporarily in the Depression and then structurally after World War II to concerns about numbers of people. This
general tendency is supplanted temporarily by specific political and
economic concerns that dislodge the powerful class themes back to
those of race and ethnic origin. While it is virtually impossible to
separate race and ethnicity from class formations in America, the
need for labor and problems with labor appear to have been a dominant force coloring population control themes in America.

Tactics, likewise, have been shaped by American realities and
strategies for success. Sterilization is used by the eugenicists as a
compulsory punitive device to save the race. This emphasis moder-
ated through the leadership of Gamble and Wood so that sterilization
comes to be seen as a normal method of birth control. Programs initiated by people like Gamble become incorporated in government
agencies; AVS conceives the voluntary approach, but with state
sponsorship. However, population controllers are not the only influence on birth control in the United States. Sterilization, when medically indicated or voluntarily planned, can stand on its own as a desirable method of permanent contraception.

One should not underestimate the influence of population control
on family-planning programs. The themes are being carried on with
new tactics, vigor, and ideological appeal by a number of organizations. The most preeminent is the Population Council.

3

"You Can't Let Nature Take Its Course": The Population Council Bridges Private Ideas to Public Policy

THIS CHAPTER examines the extent to which the population control movement continues to influence America's thinking about birth control and helps to formulate population policy. One empirical study of the population policy process in the United States finds "evidence that the discourse is dominated by a compact and identifiable coalition of public officials, private notables, and professional specialists functioning through government, private, and intellectual institutions interested in problems of population growth" (Bachrach and Bergman 1973, 602). The Population Council is at the center of this coalition.

The initial mission of the Population Council was to precipitate broadly defined population-control policies in the Third World. Its approach can be characterized as sophisticated, even enlightened, particularly in the way it attempted to cleanse population control doctrine of its traditional racist and eugenic content while maintaining the essential Malthusian goals. This look at the Population Council traces the institutional exercise of its power for the past thirty years. Grounding the objectives of the Population Council in the context of the post-WWII epoch provides the essential historical perspective. The council's documents are most informative in this respect (annual reports from 1952 through 1980, testimony, position papers, internal memos, authorized accounts, and so forth); secondary and interpretive accounts fill in some of the missing gaps.

Origins of the Population Council

In 1934, at the age of twenty-eight, John D. Rockefeller III wrote to his father that "it is in this field in which I will be interested—as I feel it is so fundamental and underlying" (Population Council 1978, 9). Rockefeller's travels throughout Asia had been important in shaping his perceptions about the problems of poverty and population growth. These concerns were reinforced after World War II.

In the late 1940s and early 1950s, birth control was a very sensitive issue, little discussed and adamantly opposed by the Catholic church. Yet Rockefeller felt the need for strong positive action. At first he sought to work through existing organizations, such as the Rockefeller Foundation. A research team, supported by the foundation to examine the relationship of population and human welfare, concentrated on the complex interaction between social change and the threat of political upheaval. This 1950 report concluded that an important goal should be "to reduce human fertility so that growth can be kept to the least dangerous level possible" (Population Council 1978, 10). Strategically acknowledging the sensitivity of existing organizations (including the Rockefeller Foundation) and governments to the issue of birth control, Rockefeller began to explore new ways to approach the problem. He consulted with Frank Notestein, a world famous demographer and director of the Office of Population Research at Princeton, and Lewis Strauss, a former Wall Street banker and associate of Laurance Rockefeller. They decided to convene a nationwide conference on population problems. This idea was discussed with Detlev Bronk, president of the Rockefeller Institute, who at the time was also president of the National Academy of Sciences. A conference was held in Williamsburg, Virginia, under the auspices of the National Academy and was supported by John D. Rockefeller III, with Bronk serving as chairman.

The conference was convened in June of 1952. Its objective was to "consider available facts and conflicting views about the effects of population growth on human welfare to the end that it may be possible to reach conclusions stimulating thought and perhaps action" (Population Council 1978, 13). The need for an organization specifically established as a catalytic agent in the population field was repeatedly emphasized. A resolution empowered the chairman to search out the organizational possibilities. The Rockefeller imprint was immediately visible: of the thirty-one conference participants thirteen were officers, fellows, trustees, or associates of Rockefeller interests or organizations. Others attending included family friends, interested parties, and a judicious sprinkling of academics. Only three women attended, which is odd in that population planning is essentially about women having babies.

In late 1952, buoyed by the Williamsburg conference, John D. Rockefeller III founded the Population Council. The council's first trustees were Rockefeller; Frank Notestein; Frederick Osborn (previously described as a member of a capitalist-class family having deep roots in the eugenics movement), secretary of the American Eugenics Society from 1928 to 1971; Thomas Parran, a distinguished Catholic layman, trustee of the Rockefeller Foundation, and an officer of assorted Mellon family foundations; Detlev Bronk, president of the Rockefeller Institute; Karl T. Compton, chairman of the corporation, Massachusetts Institute of Technology, trustee of the Ford Foundation, and director of various corporations; and Lewis Strauss, former secretary of Commerce, financial advisor to Laurance Rockefeller, director of RCA, NBC, the Rockefeller Center, and soon to be chairman of the Atomic Energy Commission. This organization took as its charge the claim that "the relation of population to material and cultural resources of the world presents one of the most critical and urgent problems of the day" (Population Council 1978, 6).

John D. Rockefeller III, the Ford Foundation, and the Rockefeller Brothers Fund were the chief benefactors of the Population Council. In its first three years of operation, the council received $1,893,000 from John D. Rockefeller and $600,000 from the Ford Foundation. In 1955 the Rockefeller Brothers Fund pledged $120,000 annually for the next three years. These gifts made possible a budget of about $500,000 for the first few years of operation. The council would enjoy the continued generous support of Rockefeller and Ford monies. For the first three years, to broaden its base within the business community, its four-member finance committee included the treasurers of American Telephone and Telegraph and General Electric, and the director of economic research for Continental Can Company.

The Population Council had an auspicious beginning—a coupling of considerable upper-class support led by two of America's most influential families and impeccable academic credentials. The grand objective of the council was to bring about a world-wide policy of population control. But why was the Population Council necessary? The ideas it espoused certainly were not new, and it was not the only organization concerned with population.

Eugenics had been undermined by two sources in the 1930s and 1940s. Within the field of genetics there were important scientific counterarguments (the Hardy-Weinberg Law) to the Mendelian one-gene-one-trait concept embraced by eugenicists, thus the "scientific" underpinning of racist eugenic ideas began to decay. But the death knell of old eugenics was sounded more by Hitler's use of once-favored arguments for sterilization and racial purity than by advances in genetic knowledge (Gould 1981). These developments discredited the eugenics movement, making its practitioners look like crackpot realists, and many capitalist-class benefactors withdrew their support. From these developments alone it was clear that a new scientific basis needed to be established if the grand Malthusian concept was to survive with any credibility.The transition from eugenics to population control was made between 1930 and 1950.

The historical context presented an additional reason for action. Earlier eugenic concerns were aimed overwhelmingly at the poor and minorities in the United States. Yet, there was a clear need for labor, which immigration fulfilled. After World War II, however, world population growth received increased attention from America. Eugenic arguments that had emphasized the danger to America from ethnic and racial minorities gave way to tenets of societal development, economic growth, international political stability, and preserving limited resources. American capital dominated the world after World War II, its competitors devastated or weakened by war. International stability, reconstruction, and economic growth were necessary to bring about world-wide prosperity and peace. The global concerns of American business leaders and policy elites were important because America had emerged as the dominant force on the world scene. The prevailing idea was that nations would handicap their economic "take-off" because population growth would constantly erode economic growth. Since "overpopulation" was said to exacerbate social unrest, diminishing the number of potentially dissatisfied people could minimize the possibilities of political instability. These ideas became a dominant influence in anchoring policy considerations. The need to establish population studies as a respectable science and, more important, to persuade governments to adopt a population policy attained a degree of urgency.

While these concerns influenced U.S foreign policy, a similar consciousness was being constructed, which would apply the same analyses and solutions to what came to be seen as similar problems in the United States. Council president, Frederick Osborn, the same man who thought the Nazi sterilization program was an excellent and important experiment, stated that overpopulation in both rich and poor nations would be a future source of instability. Thus the council also sought to "discourage births among the socially handicapped" in the United States (cited in Weissman 1970, 44). The Population Council was straightforward about the impact it wanted to have on the United States. Its 1958 annual report, written under Osborn's tutelage, stated that "even in the United States, present rates of growth may well handicap education and cultural advances and make more difficult the adjustments to the rapid rate of urbanization" (Population Council 1958, 5–6).

A goal of the Population Council was to construct a more legitimate variant on an old Malthusian theme. The organizational and ideological tasks were the creation of an organization to resolve the problem of limiting population growth. To accomplish this feat the council helped create a population establishment; forged a coalition to further its goals; attempted to influence public opinion by educating government, corporate, and academic leaders; and, throughout the world, including the United States, successfully rallied scientific and political support to institute population-control policies. It must be recognized that Rockefeller and his organization were searching for ways within their system of values to diminish human misery and to help uplift humanity. Their world view was nourished by a desire for a specific method of societal development, a fear of political upheaval, and a preference for long-term stability.

Goals and Functions of the Council

Key individuals and organizations of the upper class formed the Population Council because they foresaw it as an integral part of a larger strategy to maintain world stability. The United States also adopted a social policy of population control largely through the vanguard efforts of the council. It is important to show how theoretically required relationships were organized and structured because the actions of people in constructing social, political, and economic relationships, rather than abstract categories of historical necessity, are significant. The mechanisms of such a policy could be argued among several interested parties, but the framework, consensus, and ideological apparatus for general policy objectives were the inspiration of the council. This section critically examines precisely how they were able to succeed.

A key to achieving success was the council's patient long-term planning. Over a period of twenty years the council realized its objectives. Another key is that the Council strategically avoided association with one specific policy, focusing, instead, on general policy formulation. Bernard Berelson, council president from 1968 to 1974, aptly put forth this view of the primary objective in an internal memorandum shortly after taking office in 1968:

> The central purpose of the Council, I take it, is not to develop demography as a scientific or academic discipline (even less, public health or reproductive physiology) nor to "solve the population problem." Rather, it is to develop sound knowledge and knowledgeable people to guide intelligent policy in the population field. We are not here "to do the job"—but *we are here to develop the scientific information, the technical plans, the training programs, and the profes-*

sional personnel that will be available for "doing the job" in the population field, however that is responsibly defined [cited in Population Council 1978, 80–81, emphasis added].

The council's patience and strategic outlook, along with its capitalist-class support, accounts to a large degree for its dominant influence on the population policy process in the United States. Over a period of twenty-five years the council accomplished four major objectives. First, a framework for a broad-range policy consensus was put into place. Second, a fundamental ideological commitment was nurtured, built on the notion of improving the quality of life by controlling population growth. State intervention would be necessary to insure effective results. The state was penetrating so many other areas of social life that intervention in birth control appeared to be just one more logical extension. Third, a popular consciousness about the need for population policy was also encouraged. Fourth, private wealth was used to generate a public obligation to further the interests of those with wealth and power.

The Population Council realized these objectives by developing a scientific network, facilitating technological advances in promising areas, and focusing on enactment of a social policy. It should be remembered that the council's activities were aimed primarily at the developing world, but in the process a dual focus emerged. This section highlights the council's efforts as they affected the United States.

A Population Establishment

The council did not espouse any particular form of population policy; rather, it "sought to encourage greater understanding of population issues throughout the world" (Population Council 1978, 25). During its first twenty-five years the council made possible a virtual reconstruction of population studies. A network of scientifically trained population professionals was developed. Personnel were connected through interlocking institutions, government offices, private foundations, university posts, and journals. Linda Gordon identifies the nexus of Rockefeller, Osborne, Princeton, Population Association of America, Milbank Memorial Fund, Office of Population Research, and Population Council as vitally important in establishing this network (Gordon, 1976). Key personnel and benefactors shuttled from one organization to another. By 1977 the council had awarded fellowships to 994 men and women, 187 of whom were from North America. This funding sparked a significant impetus in mobilizing the professionals to action. The universities and the profession needed financial support and moral encouragement to take up the sensitive issues. Professional and academic norms were influenced from the respectable base of the council, as was a specific problem-oriented approach to population studies.

The impact of the council's fellowship program on the field of population studies should not be underestimated. In fact, the council likes to boast about the observation of an outside evaluator who, after taking stock of the field in 1974, wrote: "Today the roster of the fellows reads like a 'Who's Who in Population' with a sizeable percentage of academic demographers tracing their professional origins to the Council's training effort. Measured against its original goals, this effort would have to be rated an almost unqualified success" (cited in Population Council 1978, 27). Hence, when American public attention turned to population dilemmas and ecological concerns (cited in Population Council 1978, 27). Hence, when American public attention turned to population dilemmas and ecological concerns in the late 1960s and early 1970s, population specialists were already deployed, largely as a consequence of the council's investment in the 1950s and 1960s.

The council not only inaugurated a generous fellowship program, but, more important, also generously contributed to research and training programs in population studies at universities in the United States. Assistance for demographic studies and conferences was provided to Columbia, Princeton, Cornell, Boston University, the University of Chicago, the University of Pennsylvania, and about two hundred other universities. Grants were made to the Milbank Memorial Fund, the Population Association of America, and various other institutions. This institution collaboration provided the basis for a continuing network of expertise. The council's intent was not to buy a group of experts; rather, its broader aim was to advance knowledge and methodology in the field. Nonetheless, its impact was to structure subtly and effectively the nature of the problems that scholars investigated, as well as to channel career patterns consistent with the council's general interests. Its effect in restructuring professional behavior can be seen in the case of the National Committee on Maternal Health. In the late 1940s, this group refused to associate openly with the "messy," controversial contraceptive work of Planned Parenthood; yet, in need of money in 1957, it accepted a sizable grant from the council to research and evaluate various methods of birth control. Its staff and activities in 1967 were subsumed under the council—"a classic example of professional cooptation," as one observer remarked (Piotrow 1973, 14).

Seminars and conferences provide a setting where interested members can become better informed by taking part in discussions with academics. Forums facilitate ongoing contacts and personnel interchanges; recruitment of academics for government, corporate, and foundation service; and socialization into the general values of population control.

Dissemination of information is a related aspect of the council's work. It has published several journals and serials, including *Studies in Family Planning*, *Current Publications in Population/Family Planning*, and *Population and Development Review*. In addition, the council has supported the publication of over fifty books in the field. Since the end of World War II the field of population studies has been largely rejuvenated and vastly enlarged, setting into motion a network of expertise and interlocking institutions that provides the intellectual and organizational basis for population control.

The establishment of a credible, scientific field of population studies was crucial to the council's perception of the importance of the issues involved. It is interesting to note how the council defines its approach as "scientific" and "noncontroversial," which is in sharp contrast to the way it labels other approaches as "emotional" and "ideological."

There is an opportunity here not only to disseminate knowledge, but
to forestall an emotional approach to the complex and potentially explosive problems of population. The science of demography deals
with the quantitative analysis of measurable units. Its findings, like
those of any scientific inquiry, present demonstrable facts. These can
provide a noncontroversial approach to human problems. Such an approach is particularly important to the solution of problems of world
population and the population problems of individual countries. An
emotional or ideological approach could rapidly turn questions of
population into highly divisive issues, and postpone their solution to a
distant future when it would be too late to avert disaster. The scientific approach lays a base for the understanding of population problems by the intellectual groups [Population Council, 1978: 6–7].

Technological Advances

The council also geared up the machinery that would provide the
necessary technological advances. Biomedical work was sponsored
to increase the understanding of the human reproductive system and
to spur technologically efficient methods of contraception. While the
council avoids the role of advocate in specific programs, its interpretation of necessities is inevitably reflected in its programs. The
council's activities and grants reveal a wide range of substantive activities and the importance attached to the development of efficient
and inexpensive contraceptive apparatuses. Council-supported projects have included female contraceptive implants, vaginal rings, in-
jectable contraception for women, a weekly pill, a monthly menses-
inducing pill, sterilization techniques and equipment, postcoital
pills, and male contraceptive implants; in addition, field testing and
clinical evaluation of contraceptive and hormonal devices have been
arranged. The council has played a major role in the development,
clinical testing, statistical evaluation, manufacture, and distribution
of modern forms of the intrauterine device (IUD). Just as technological developments have been strongly influenced in any society
by the class that is in power, so too are patriarchal interests embodied in the search for scientific solutions. Many needed advances are
aimed at women.

Demonstration and training programs were sponsored as a logical corollary to stimulating technological advancements. A Philadelphia group, for instance, was the recipient of grants in the late 1960s to service "disadvantaged groups" (blacks). In the late 1960s, as part of a larger international program, the council subsidized a postpartum family-planning demonstration program in seven U.S. hospitals servicing poor and minority clients: Los Angeles County General, Harlem, Wayne County, Department of Public Health, Washington, D.C., and others. Family-planning training and service programs were made feasible by council monies in 1971. A symbiotic relationship evolved between the council and government agencies: the Office for Economic Opportunity; Health, Education, and Welfare; the National Institutes of Health; and the Agency for International Development. The Council began receiving large amounts of federal money in the mid-1960s, some of which was used to set up programs the government considered too sensitive for its own agencies, such as demonstration projects that included sterilization. Providing incentive to enable technological breakthroughs and technical assistance was the second major aspect of the council's venture to integrate a population-control framework into existing institutions.

Population Policy

The third goal, crucial to achieving the council's long-range objectives, was the most complex and difficult: establishing the necessity for a population policy. By the mid-1960s a network of population experts had been created, technological advances such as the IUD and the pill had been spurred, and demonstration and training programs were already foreshadowing the practical applications. The prerequisites for a population policy had been met. In 1968 the council began to broaden its "interest in long-run considerations of population policy." The focus switched to "give more direct, explicit, and sustained attention to the varied problems of population policy" (Population Council, 1968, 14–15).

How to awaken the nation to the population crisis looming on the horizon was a major problem. Newspaper items, magazine articles, and public discourse over several years started to instill this realization. A stunning reversal of media coverage occurred in 1959; before then the number of articles and general coverage was minimal, but rising. From 1959 on, however, media attention was fixed on population control and birth control, as indicated by the number of entries listed under "contraception" in *The Readers Guide To Periodicals*. Between 1950 and 1954 forty articles were listed, but from 1960 to 1964 the number jumped to over three hundred. Similarly, in 1954 5 inches were devoted to "population" in the *New York Times Index*; by 1965 coverage increased to 26.5 inches (Piotrow 1973).

The atmosphere surrounding public discussion of birth control changed rapidly in 1959. The president's committee to study the U.S. assistance program (Draper Committee) specified solutions to the "population explosion," which was considered a threat to international stability. In the same year, a State Department review of population trends warned, "Rapid population growth may prove to be one of the greatest obstacles to . . . maintenance of political stability in many areas of the world" (cited in Piotrow 1973, 42). Foreign-policy pressures, spurred by the Population Council, put public discussion of birth control in a new context and helped to break the media silence on contraceptive issues. Other pressures were mounting as well. The World Council of Churches approved a report strongly justifying all birth-control methods; and four major religious groups in the United States endorsed family planning. Furthermore, the American Public Health Association recommended that birth control be made an integral part of health programs.

Birth control, once considered too sensitive for public attention, came into the spotlight of national publicity at the end of 1959. Catholic bishops of the United States denounced government assistance, either at home or abroad, for contraception. John F. Kennedy, a Catholic, was running for the presidency in 1960, and his candidacy generated a flurry of political activity on the issue of birth control. The news media awakened to the issue and placed it on the agenda for coverage (Piotrow 1973). Because of the "sexual revolution" of the 1960s, sex and contraception remained lively issues for national attention.

This media awakening soon escalated into a campaign of sensationalism. A program of domestic propaganda to alarm the public was inaugurated in 1967 by the Campaign to Check the Population Explosion, a group that sponsored a series of one-and two-page ads appearing in the *New York Times*, the *Washington Post, Fortune*, the *Wall Street Journal, Harpers, Time*, and *Saturday Review* from 1968 to 1970. Hugh Moore, who at the time was also president of the Association for Voluntary Sterilization, was the prime mover in this campaign. The signers of these ads drew upon a few important trustees and financial patrons of the Population Council, such as Strauss, Bronk, Mrs. Albert Lasker, Mrs. Cordelia Scaife May, and Eugene Black. More important, perhaps, is that these ads attracted the Mellons, Duponts, McCormicks, Vanderbilts, Cabots, and Tafts. Of the 139 signers of these alarmist ads only nine were women (Lader 1971). Rockefeller felt that scare tactics emphasizing slogans like "population bomb" or "population explosion" might create an atmosphere of panic; thus he was never associated with these ads. Nonetheless, the ads represent an embracing of population control solutions by wide segments of the upper class. While the Campaign to Check the Population Explosion focused on cruder domestic propaganda, the council became involved in education in its own limited way. Among other things, they sponsored speakers and distributed films (one starred a Walt Disney character talking about family planning). One film, *The Costly Crowd*, which was available at no charge, is described as being

> geared specifically to businessmen or persons of upper level affluence
> involved in community problems, the film shows community plan-
> ning in action as a group considers schools, transportation, hospitals,
> and other municipal needs. The realization grows among the planners
> that all projects—traffic, sanitation, roads, police, fire, courts, jail—
> will be quickly outmoded. The "hero" planner drives past slums
> filled with unwanted children, crime, narcotics, and welfare cost. The
> planner-businessman finally realized that the increased population he

is counting on to be producers and consumers will turn out to be just
more poor people who are unable to pay taxes, and who are a liability
on society rather than contributors to the social fabric. It becomes
suddenly clear to him: you can't let nature take its course [Zatuchini
1970, 439].

Despite these side ventures into public education, the council primarily attended to providing expertise and guiding policy. In the
mid-1960s, council officers and representatives began testifying before congressional committees on population and family-planning issues. They consistently urged the adoption of family-planning programs and the extension of related health services. Thus they became
advocates of *all* forms of birth control, including abortion, birth
control pills, sterilization, and sex education. An alliance among
the Population Council, Planned Parenthood, liberals, and various
women's organizations emerged on the issue of making services
available to those who could not afford them. The issue of birth control availability galvanized a broad coalition, even though the reasons underlying the cooperation were vastly different. Nonetheless,
advocates of women's rights, population controllers, liberals, and
even eugenicists rallied around the issue. The basis of the coalition
was the argument that poor people should have access to the same
services already available to the middle class. Expansion of the state
into new territories was an accepted approach to solving many societal problems. Those opposing extension of services were the
Right-to-Life movement and the Catholic church—opponents of all
forms of birth control. The equal-opportunity premise of extending
birth-control services to the needy became the basis of a coalition that propelled population-control programs into widespread
existence.

The view that state-imposed sanctions must be a necessary part
of any program to achieve population stability was dreaded by some
government officials and planners. Programs that promised social
stability through the elimination of "unwanted" fertility seemed to
reassure the public that the state would not regulate reproduction.

The chief selling points became the "right to choose," translated practically to mean access to services for the poor, and this became its ultimate ideological end. Frank Notestein, a founder, past president and trustee of the council, and noted demographer, hailed federal intervention into family planning as "a new and important freedom in the world. . . . It is a matter of major importance that this kind of new freedom, now existing for the bulk of the population be extended to its most disadvantaged parts" (Notestein 1970, 448–51). Five million women were initially defined as being at high risk for unwanted pregnancy, and these women, concentrated among the poor and minorities, became the target of government policy.

Historical conditions were conducive to a full-fledged commitment to population policy; however, government leaders had to be persuaded of the timeliness, wisdom, logic and efficacy for such a policy. The work of John D. Rockefeller III again took center stage. At his persistent urging, President Johnson, in 1968, appointed the Committee on Population and Family Planning, which Rockefeller co-chaired. The committee proposed a commission to assess the consequences of population trends in the United States, to evaluate progress in the fledgling family programs already in operation, and to consider alternative population policies. The leadership, expertise, and perspective of the council was embodied in the committee's proposals.

Under President Nixon the influence of Rockefeller and the council did not diminish. The first presidential message on population was delivered by Nixon to Congress in 1969, and it was strongly flavored with the committee's recommendations. Nixon was already on record as saying "the frightening fact is that the poor are multiplying twice as fast as the rich" (cited in Lappe and Collins 1977, 4). He was now ready to commit the nation to supporting family-planning programs that defined the population problem as unwanted children in poor families. In the presidential message, Nixon proclaimed that the nation should "establish as a national goal the provision of adequate family planning services within the next five years to all those who want them but cannot afford them" (cited in Piotrow 1973, 169).

His effort to adopt a five-year plan on population policy was completed in 1970 with the passage of the Family Planning Services and
Research Act. Priority was given to low-income families.

Nixon appointed a blue-ribbon Commission on Population Growth
and the American Future, which Rockefeller also headed. Representatives from corporate and financial worlds, foundations, universities, and the Population Council dominated the commission's
makeup, although youth, blacks, and women were represented. The
commission's final report in 1972 is a strong declaration for population control, a final legitimation of policies already underway, and
concludes that slowing population growth would be wise policy.
Recommendations included freer access to birth-control information
and services, elimination of restrictions on sterilization, and liberalized abortion laws. Several commission members dissented from
these recommendations, and Nixon balked at some of the most controversial ones, such as abortion and contraceptive information and
services for teenagers. These were most distasteful to Catholics,
members of Right to Life, and the emerging New Right.

Nixon's response to the report disappointed advocates of population control, and others, but this should not be seen as the sole criteria of its effectiveness. The director of the commission, Charles
Westoff, argued that the report has been prominent in subsequent activities of Congress and various government agencies responsible for
family planning and related issues. He also points to the lasting educational benefits and international impact of the report. He wrote that
the commission "represented an important effort by an advanced
country to develop a national population policy—the basic thrust of
which was to slow growth in order to maximize the 'quality of life'"
(Westoff 1975, 59). Rockefeller capsulized the enduring importance
of the report's legitimating function when he testified in 1972 that in
the United States "there are no substantial benefits to be gained from
continued population growth. In fact, the results of our research indicate the growth we have experienced in the past twenty years has
aggravated many of the nation's problems and made their solutions
more difficult" (U.S. Senate Committee on Appropriations 1972,
5,647).

Equal access to services, which were guaranteed and provided by the government, and concerns over the "quality of life" were the ideological basis upon which an extension of population policy was grounded. The emerging consensus was that the government could improve the quality of life by controlling unwanted fertility. The same day Nixon signed the bill expanding family planning and creating a federal office to coordinate methods of population-growth control, the *New York Times* reported that "the White House also announced that Mr. Nixon had vetoed a bill that would have set up a three-year $255 million program to train family doctors" (*New York Times*, 1970). The signed bill might reduce future costs to the public by lowering the birth rate of the poor, but the vetoed bill might have improved the health and life chances of those already born. Concentrating on population growth as the main obstacle to a better life further obfuscates the more fundamental question of inequalities in the distribution of wealth. Seen this way, population policy is an example of victim blaming at the system level—pollution, hunger, crime, disease are portrayed as a product of too many people rather than a social consequence of the private accumulation of wealth and private decisions about how to use resources.

The Social System of Support for Population Control

Over the years the council's board of trustees has reflected widespread support within the upper class and corporate elite. Its finance committee, for instance, has always provided a direct linkage to the core of corporate and financial capital. Chief among its patrons, in addition to Ford and Rockefeller, have been the Hechts, Cordelia May, the Scaifes, and the Kresge, Mellon and Mott Foundations. The council's benefactors are listed in Figure 3-1.

If they are interested in public legitimation, policy-formation groups must appear to have a broad base of support, a notion on which the council consciously acted. From the outset Rockefeller made sure the board of trustees had prestigious academic representatives. In the late 1970s, he sought to expand the base of the board to include women, minorities, and international representatives.

FIGURE 3-1
Major Private Sources of Council Funds, 1952–1979

Vivian B. Allen		Cordelia S. May	508,000
Foundation	$ 1,338,000	Cordelia S. May Chari-	
Avalon Foundation	200,000	table Trust	21,000,000
Carnegie Corporation of		The Andrew W. Mellon	
New York	120,000	Foundation	5,000,000
Robert Sterling Clark		Charles Stewart Mott	
Foundation	27,000	Foundation	29,000
The Commonwealth Fund	915,000	Rockefeller Family and	
The Ford Foundation	63,000,000	Foundations	49,000,000
Freda E. and George J.		The Rosenstock	
Hecht	1,670,000	Foundation	6,000
Independence Foundation	350,000	Salisbury Community	
The Kresge Foundation	800,000	Foundation	7,500
The John and Mary R.		Alfred P. Sloan	
Markle Foundation	20,000	Foundation	10,000
Abby R. Mauze	$ 2,486,000	Mr. and Mrs. John	
		Spencer	195,000

Murray D. Buxbaum

Mrs. James M. Faulkner

Robert W. Gillespie

Gleich Foundation

John A. Harris IV

Thomas C. Hayes

The Hecht–*Parents* Magazine Foundation for Child Welfare

The W. R. Hewlett Foundation

George Frederick Jewett Foundation

Larned Johnson Foundation

Albert and Mary Lasker Foundation

John Lindsley Fund

Jack Lippes

Stewart R. Mott

Stewart R. Mott Charitable Trust

The New York Community Trust (Community Funds)

Frederick Osborn

Planned Parenthood Federation of America

The Prospect Hill Foundation of America

Ritchie H. Reed Fellowship Fund

Adaline P. Satterthwaite

Mrs. Alan M. Scaife and Family

Scaife Family Charitable Trusts

Scheinman, Hochstin, and Trotta Foundation

The William Lightfoot Schultz Foundation

Smith, Kline, and French Foundation

The Tinker Foundation

W. T. Weber

William C. Whitney Foundation

The Windsor Foundation

Dewitt Wallace Foundation

Source: Population Council 1978, 163; Population Council Annual Reports 1958–1979.
    For those for whom dollars figures are not given, donations were less than $5,000.

Rockefeller deserves credit for his foresight in seeing the need to sustain the credibility of the organization. Increased government financing, along with pressure from women's groups and minorities, influenced the council to broaden its board. When Rockefeller died in 1978 his vision for the council had been largely realized. He had removed himself from the active day-to-day operations long before his death—in fact, professional leadership had been managing the organization for twenty years. Over this period, as some might anticipate, one can witness the bureaucratization and rationalization of a rapidly expanding organization. The personal charisma of Rockefeller may have been routinized, but upper-class support was not. Key positions in the organization continue to be held by men from wealthy families or corporate backgrounds (finance committee, trustees, and upper-level officers). Above all, money continues to roll in; the enormous investment signifies the importance attached to its work: the Ford Foundation has supplied more than $63 million and the Rockefeller interests have chipped in over $50 million. The federal government is now able to relieve the council of some of its original functions, which may explain why the annual budget has gradually diminished over the last few years.

In a symbiotic fashion, the council supplied the groundwork for forging class consensus on the broad issue of population control while its activities were financed by a powerful upper-class sector. If the power of organizations increases with their ability to control resources and provide expertise, then the Population Council had the potential to be a dominant organization. This is not to say that there were no dissidents or that there were no substantial differences over style; as glimpsed in the Campaign to Check the Population Explosion's advertising efforts, there were both dissidents and differences. The main point is that the council acted as a leading faction to socialize the rest of the upper class into the values of population control and to recruit members into active participation.

Another indication of the council's mastery in influencing policy and gaining high-level converts is its ability to attract government financing. Starting in the mid-1960s large amounts of money from the Agency for International Development and the National Institutes of Health were allocated annually to the council. The Population Council took on aspects of a state organization because it had the expertise and ability to carry out projects for which government agencies were not equipped or direct government intervention was considered too sensitive. For the most part these were demonstration projects, which in turn further boosted the council's credentials. This symbiotic relationship not only facilitated the interchange of ideas and personnel between government and private organizations, but also shifted a part of the financing for population-control policies from elite foundations and families to government agencies. Private wealth was used to create a public commitment to foster a particular perspective. Rockefeller noted this extraordinary achievement by remarking in 1969: "I helped found the Population Council. Its present annual budget of $13 million is financed by grants from both public and private resources (at the time we started, any government participation would have been politically unthinkable)" (cited in Barclay, Enright, and Reynolds 1970, 3).

This symbiotic relationship was not limited to the Population Council. Ray Ravenholt, director of the Office of Population for the Agency for International Development, stated that A.I.D.'s most sensitive actions frequently cannot be spoken of publicly, citing, for example, the case of funds and equipment flowing into Mexico through the International Planned Parenthood Federation. Because of the political sensitivity of U.S.-sponsored population-control programs, A.I.D. finds it necessary to hide behind seemingly humanitarian international agencies for which it provides the bulk of the funding. He proudly reported that $12 million was secretly funneled to Mexico through the Association for Voluntary Sterilization, Family Planning International Assistance (part of Planned Parenthood Federation of America) and others. He describes this as a remarkably "creative action" (CARASA News 1978).

This analysis of the role of the Population Council shows how a dominant class organizes itself and then exerts its power to shape opinion and policy. The council's success can be measured by four major accomplishments. First, it helped to convince the upper class and the nation's political leaders of the wisdom in using government power to control population growth. Second, it fostered popular consciousness about the need for family-planning programs. Third, private wealth helped to shape the public commitment to population policy in such a way as to be consistent with the interests of the wealthy and powerful. Fourth, and most important, when family planning became legitimate enough for federal support, the programs that emerged were strongly influenced by population-control objectives.

These are long-range and apparently enduring achievements. Neither the specifics of application nor the programmatic details are as crucial as the enduring aspects of policy planning. While this affords the state a large degree of autonomy to design and implement specific programs, it is clear that the Population Council played the instrumental role in establishing policy parameters. The broad policy, as well as the supporting ideology, was formulated as a response both to immediate problems and to long-range concerns about systems maintenance. As will be noted in a later chapter, this helps set in motion a dynamic whereby it is in the institutional self-interests of most social service agencies to deliver family-planning programs that cut down the demand for future public services.

Bachrach and Bergman (1973) note that the exclusionary and class nature of the population-control movement suggests it is motivated by a desire to secure a future in which its members' privileged positions and life styles will be preserved and transmitted to their next generation. The history of the council vividly illustrates the capacity of a dominant class to develop this self-interest, translate that consciousness into a more generalized ideology, and formulate social policy. The long-range systemic interests of the dominant class, as perceived by "farsighted" members, were turned into the dominant social ideas, and those interests became the dominant ideas of society on the issue of family planning. The evidence indicates that older, entrenched families appeared to be more active in this endeavor. Participation in the council was aimed at formulating, advocating, and coordinating political strategy, all of which were accomplished by the council's active participation in governmental processes for the purpose of implementing its political strategy.

The active effort to shape state policy became the focus of the self-organization of the capitalist class (Zeitlin 1980).

While formalizing a model from this case is a tantalizing prospect, there are ample reasons to be cautious. Just like other policy-formation groups, the Population Council is historically specific to its epoch and its perceived mission. More important, it is atypical: consensus was relatively easy to achieve because there was no substantial intraclass friction over specific interests and the issue of population control was not an active arena for interclass conflict. Other groups were relatively weak and considerably less organized and financed. The goal was to stimulate the adoption of a broad policy; therefore, arguments over specifics could, in most instances, be easily reduced to questions of style.

The black liberation movement of the late 1960s mounted one of the few challenges to government family-planning policy. The movement denounced government-sponsored family-planning programs as racial genocide. In response, its predominantly male leadership urged black women to resist these efforts; some even urged black women to "abandon birth controls" and "to produce more babies, not less" (Bambara 1970, 163; Petchesky 1984: 130). They were confusing birth control with the aims of population control. Black women like Toni Cade Bambara and Angela Davis argued that this rhetoric and confusion ignored women's needs. Toni Cade Bambara noted the pill does not liberate women, but it "gives her choice" and is not inherently "counterrevolutionary" (Bambara 1970, 168). Angela Davis points out that equating "birth control with genocide" was "an exaggerated—even paranoic—reaction" (Davis 1981, 203). It was black, Puerto Rican, and native American women, facing the dual oppression of being minority women, who made a sharp distinction between support for birth control and opposition to population control.

There are lessons that seem especially relevant for future considerations. While historical evidence compellingly links a class-based organization to general policy objectives (and ideology), attempts to mechanically interpolate the *plans* of any group to inextricable, specific policy *outcomes* would omit entirely any role for a mediating welfare state apparatus. Such a view also neglects the potential ability of groups and organized social movements to pressure state agencies on specific issues. Furthermore, elitist organizations like the Population Council spring up to deal with identifiable sets of issues and problems and, to be effective, they sometimes make tactical alliances. Organizations abound, but alliances on different issues are susceptible to shifts.

The unique and enduring achievement of the Population Council has been to tailor old population-control ideas to new realities and to anchor them in governmental social policy. Chapter 4 focuses on what many people believe is the latest manifestation of population control in America—sterilization abuse and patterns of female sterilization.

4

Sterilization Abuse and Patterns of Female Sterilization

TWO EVENTS radically changed the status of sterilization in the United States in the early 1970s: sterilization became available to the poor, and the medical establishment liberalized its guidelines. Federally supported family-planning services had been operating since 1965, but abortion and sterilization were prohibited. In 1969 the bar against sterilization was removed. At a time when budget "belt tightening" was a byword for most government-sponsored health care programs, sterilizations were a vital part of a rapid expansion in government-supported contraceptive services.

In 1969 the medical establishment accommodated technical advances in tubal ligation procedures and the increasing popularity of sterilization practices. The American College of Obstetricians and Gynecologists (ACOG) withdrew its rule-of-thumb age-parity formula for sterilization eligibility, whereby a woman's age multiplied by the number of children she has must equal at least 120 before she can be sterilized. This formula made it difficult for women who wanted no children, or small families, to curtail their fertility. In 1970 ACOG dropped its widely used recommendation that two doctors and a psychiatrist be consulted before sterilization surgery. Thus by the early 1970s the availability (including government support) and the liberalization of guidelines insured, for the first time, that sterilization could become an effective method of birth control.

There is no doubt that millions of women have benefited from these changes.

The shift in the official status of sterilization was partly a response to its increasing acceptance, which generated an even greater popularity. There are sound reasons why the overall preference for sterilization among all women has been increasing. As technology improves and associated risks diminish, it looks more attractive as a permanent way to control fertility. More women are working now than ever before because families are unable to maintain a decent standard of living on a single wage; job opportunities can lead to employment and independence, and more women head households. About two and one-half times as many women as men work at jobs that offer only part-time or irregular employment. But since the late 1970s, the costs of a pregnancy and supporting a child make living conditions increasingly difficult, especially given the diminishing availability of programs that offer assistance to pregnant women, children, and mothers with young children. This material context would inevitably affect decisions about childbearing and contraception.

Rosalind Petchesky (1981), in her incisive analysis of female sterilization, brings into sharp focus several dimensions of cultural influence. Popular culture promotes female sterilization under the guise of sexual liberation. The prolific efforts of the Association for Voluntary Sterilization (AVS) to gain public acceptance cannot be underestimated. The sterilization trend is reinforced through the mass media, magazines, books, and songs. An appealing aspect of the notion of sexual liberation is that more freedom comes from not having to worry about unwanted pregnancies. Sterilization advocates and providers promise a quick technological fix, advertised as "band-aid surgery," to eliminate fear and tension from the sexual act and to transform the experience of sexuality.

Petchesky says there are also good reasons to believe that "sterilization may be a means of avoiding birth control for those women who are most influenced by traditional sexual relations and ideologies" (Petchesky 1981, 65). In situations where decisions about contraception are a constant dilemma or where male partners are hostile to or unwilling to take birth-control responsibilities, she reasons that women may prefer sterilization because it is less conspicuous and least dependent on male cooperation.

For Catholics, sterilization may offer an alternative to the turmoil that often accompanies the regular use of contraceptive devices and drugs. Sterilization entails one decision. Furthermore, it is the method of birth control furthest removed from sexual planning and practices. The church has been doctrinaire and publicly vociferous on abortion; its position on sterilization has been relatively muted. Church influence may translate into practice, as one study reveals a trend toward convergence on prevalence of sterilization when comparing Catholics and non-Catholics. Catholic reliance on sterilization began to increase substantially after 1970 (Westoff and Jones 1977b). Thus there are sound material and cultural reasons underlying the rising popularity of sterilization among *all* women. The social context of reproductive choice and the experience of birth control vary drastically for different groups of women. The same changed status of sterilization that has benefited so many women may well have left the floodgates to abuse wide open for others.

Federal programs encouraged a comparatively risky procedure that could prematurely curtail a woman's fertility, even though at first there were no safeguards against abuse, which, according to the record, was common. Women often were misled about the dangers of surgery; misinformed about its permanence; coerced while under the stress of labor or abortion; led to believe that other medical or social services like child delivery, abortion, or welfare benefits would be withheld; and sometimes were uninformed that they had been sterilized. Several widely publicized lawsuits and numerous reports between 1973 and 1976 speak to the character and widespread nature of the abuse. A review of these cases can provide insight into the consequences of an unmonitored program and identify the groups most susceptible to abuse.

Lawsuits, Abuses, and Violations

Most notorious, perhaps, is the case of the Relf sisters. In June 1973, Mary Alice, then twelve, and Minnie, then fourteen, were sterilized in a Montgomery, Alabama hospital under the auspices of a project funded by OEO, the agency designated to fight the war on poverty. On June 13, the family-planning nurse who picked up Mrs. Relf and her two youngest daughters told Mrs. Relf that the girls had to go to the doctor's office for shots. From the doctor's office they were taken to the hospital, where Mary Alice and Minnie were assigned rooms. Mrs. Relf, unable to read or write, put her mark on a piece of paper and was then escorted home. She had no idea she had just signed a consent form authorizing sterilization surgery. Mrs. Relf said she "put an X on a piece of paper" because the nurse "told me that they were going to give them some shots." The next morning Mary Alice and Minnie were placed under general anesthetic and sterilized. No physician had discussed with the girls or their parents the nature and consequences of the surgery—and the family had not asked for family-planning assistance. Instead, as one welfare official explained, they were sought out for sterilization because boys were "hanging around" the girls. Welfare officials also believed the girls lacked the "mental talents" to take the pill. Incidentally, an older sister, Katie, age sixteen, had locked herself in her room and refused to go when the family-planning nurse returned for her later the same day (U.S. Senate Subcommittee on Health 1973; *New York Times Index 1973* 1974).

In Aiken County, South Carolina, three physicians agreed among themselves to refuse to deliver a third child to mothers receiving welfare without their consent to simultaneous postpartum sterilization. A subsequent investigation revealed that one doctor had performed twenty-eight such sterilizations in six months. His nurse, trying to assure the public that the sterilizations were not racially motivated, said: "This is not a civil rights thing, or a racial thing, it is just welfare" (Caress 1975, 11).

Ten Mexican-American women, one of whom was Guadalupe Acosta, sued the Los Angeles County Hospital for obtaining consent in English when they spoke only Spanish. The women, while in labor or under anesthesia, agreed to the procedure; one was even denied a pain-killing medication until she consented. Four of the women did not learn they had been sterilized until after they sought birth-control devices. One woman did not become aware of her sterilization until four years later during a medical examination. They lost their civil suit, *Madrigal v. Quilligan*, because the judge saw the problem as "essentially the result of a breakdown in communication between the patients and the doctors." He conceded that "there is no doubt but that these women have suffered severe emotional and physical stress," but he ruled "one can hardly blame the doctors" (cited in Velez 1978).

Adverse publicity from the Relf case and pressure from reproductive rights groups led to the institution of guidelines in 1974, which, although prepared in 1972, had been ignored for over twenty-two months. The Department of Health, Education, and Welfare imposed a moratorium on sterilizing people under twenty-one and issued regulations to ensure that sterilizations be voluntary. In addition, Judge Gesell, in *Relf v. Weinberger et al.* (1974), barred federally-funded sterilization of minors and ordered that the existing regulation be amended to protect persons legally capable of consenting from being intimidated or coerced. In Aiken County, South Carolina, the offending doctor was decertified by HEW and barred from providing obstetrical services for Medicaid money, although he was allowed to receive federal grants for gynecological services to indigent patients.

From these three cases, and many others like them, precipitated the following issue: are these extraordinary, isolated cases of abuse subject to remedy or are they the surface layer of a much deeper phenomenon? Several reports based on institutionwide practices reveal that the individual abuses were more than merely isolated or aberrant cases.

The General Accounting Office investigated four of the twelve districts serviced by the Indian Health Service (IHS) and found that 3,406 native American women had been sterilized by the IHS between 1973 and 1976. The report stated that the women had not been informed about either the permanence of the operation or other birth-control options. The study did not reveal blatant coercion, but it did suggest that Indian women may have thought they had to agree to the operation (U.S. General Accounting Office 1976). Extrapolating from this report, and citing her own data, Connie Uri claims that up to one-fourth of native American women of childbearing age have been sterilized. One startling example of abuse occurred at the IHS hospital in Claremore, Oklahoma: 194 sterilizations were performed in one year—one out of every four women admitted to the hospital. Four of these women were under twenty years old (*Medical Tribune* 1977).

A survey of surgical sterilizations in American and Canadian teaching hospitals showed compulsory sterilization to be endemic in North American teaching hospitals. The study reported that in one-third to two-thirds of the hospitals, "Some women desiring an abortion were required to have a simultaneous sterilization as a condition of approval of the abortion. . . . In all, 53.6 percent of teaching hospitals made this requirement for some of their patients" (Eliot et al. 1970, 93). It is probable that the rate is even higher, since the practice was illegal and, hence, likely to be underreported. Coupling abortion to sterilization for indigent patients, known as the "package deal," makes the sterilization less than voluntary.

The Health Research Group issued a report in 1973 that documented enormous increases in the use of female sterilization over a two-year period in selected teaching hospitals. The Women's Hospital of the Los Angeles County Medical Center, for example, showed a 470 percent increase in tubal ligations. The report claimed that these operations were being "sold" by surgeons in a manner not unlike deceptive advertising. "Pushing" and "hard-selling" sterilizations were common practice; one teaching resident told incoming interns "to ask every one of the girls if they want their tubes tied, regardless of how old they are." The report speculated that at least "several hundred thousand are considerably less than well informed when they decide to be sterilized" (Rosenfeld et al. 1973, 7).

A prudent conclusion from these reports is that the cases of Minnie and Mary Alice Relf and Guadalupe Acosta were not isolated instances of ill treatment by irresponsible doctors or welfare officials. Prior to safeguards, abuses were widespread. The 1974 guidelines, strengthened by court order, went into effect to prevent the occurrence of further abuses. Two seemingly contradictory processes were put into motion; the guidelines were largely ignored, but the worst abuses began to decline.

According to a study by the American Civil Liberties Union (ACLU) in 1974, few major teaching hospitals followed the HEW regulations. When the regulations were half a year old, questionnaires were sent to the heads of 154 teaching hospitals. Of the less than one-third who bothered to reply, only one in three indicated that they were in compliance. The report stated that thirty-six major teaching hospitals were not complying with federal regulations on sterilization (Krauss 1975).

Nine months after the court-ordered regulation went into effect, the Health Research Group issued a report that corroborated the ACLU findings. Three-quarters of the hospitals were still violating the regulations; one-third were completely unaware of the legal requirements. "It is probable that 3,600 U.S. hospitals are presently out of compliance with the federal regulations," the study reported. It went on to say that "HEW had apparently not made the slightest effort to inform hospitals of their obligation" (McGarrah 1975, 4).

Five years after the original regulations went into effect, and just before they were revised, the Health Research Group issued another follow-up report on hospital compliance. Seven out of ten hospitals performing Medicaid sterilizations still violated the 1974 rules. Only 30 percent of the eighty-three responding hospitals were found to be in full compliance. Procedures designed to eliminate pressure on indigent Medicaid recipients to be sterilized—prohibition on obtaining consent during labor, a mandated waiting period, and the policy of informing a woman that no benefits will be lost if she is not sterilized—were violated. The prohibition against sterilizing minors was also violated (Bogue and Sigelman 1979).

In 1981, more than seven years after the original regulations and more than two years since their revision, the Health Research Group, in yet another report, found the situation essentially unchanged. Based on data submitted by state Medicaid programs and Health and Human Services (formerly HEW) inspector general state audits, the report revealed that many states persisted in violating federal regulations on low-income Medicaid patients (Sigelman 1981).

From the cases and reports already cited it is palpably clear not only that abuse remains a problem but also that the remedy of guidelines remains ineffective because noncompliance with regulations appears to be routine. Yet it is evident that after 1974 the number of flagrant abuses has diminished.

Patterns of Sterilization

Historically, sterilization has been advocated for eugenic purposes. Controversy still rages over whether the initial abuses in federal programs were isolated occurrences that could be remedied with stricter monitoring or whether they represented the visible layer of a deeper and more persistent pattern. This public controversy has been argued largely on the basis of the qualitative data, lawsuits, and anecdotal information already cited (Donovan 1976). Without a solid empirical foundation, however, many important questions remain unaddressed. Other things being equal, are poor and minority women more likely to be sterilized, aided by federal financial participation, than other women in the population? Examination of concrete results should help to explain actual historical developments. In the following section, the few existing studies on sterilization will be reviewed. Next, new data will be presented—facts that stand in contrast with extant studies and shed new light on an old debate.[1]

To test the argument of possible discrimination, one must look at sterilization among relevant subgroups. Literature, to date, says that there is virtually no discrimination in sterilization practices. One characteristic study concludes that in rates of sterilization, ethnic groups and welfare clients "are not disproportionately represented" (Vaughan and Sparer 1974, 229). But this literature has serious flaws.

Available studies are based on samples ill matched to answer questions about possible discrimination; they are poorly designed, and data bear indirectly on sterilization. Typically, samples are limited to whites or married couples, or both, thus aggregate discrimination against minorities or welfare recipients is impossible to detect. For example, one of the best works on sterilization, by Bumpass and Presser, uses a sample that reports only on married women currently living with their spouses (Bumpass and Presser 1972). Thus, there are no data on single mothers, women receiving welfare, and divorced women. Another study reports on a sample of women in federal family-planning services (Vaughan and Sparer 1974); another is limited to white, married women (Westoff and Jones 1977a); and still another reports only on married couples (U.S. Department of Health, Education, and Welfare 1978). One study did report that nonwhites and the medically indigent were sterilized at higher rates than other women (Lewit 1973). After standardizing for age and parity a 20 percent differential remained. But this study is severely limited because it only examined the sterilizations of those who concomitantly had abortions. Because reliable literature is scarce, one can conclude that data sources and methodologies are inadequate. A compelling or reliable conclusion requires a more appropriate data source.

Data and Method

Data from the National Survey of Family Growth (NSFG), Cycles I and II, consist of personal interviews with civilian, noninstitutionalized women living in the continental United States, who were between fifteen and forty-five years of age at the time of the survey and were married, divorced, separated, single and living with their own children, or widowed. The only women of childbearing age not sampled were single women without children. Field work for Cycle I was conducted in September 1973 and consisted of 9,797 interviews. Cycle II, conducted in April 1976, included 8,611 respondents. This survey contains the most appropriate, available information upon which to construct prevalence patterns for sterilization. This excellent data source has been used to examine broad sterilization trends only in a few instances, and these sparse studies focus on married couples as the unit of analysis, excluding precisely those groups that should be examined (Ford 1978; Westoff and McCarthy 1979).

This analysis entails an examination of the incidence of contraceptive sterilizations as they vary across subgroups in the populations. Key variables include minority status, poverty status, welfare status, and parity.[2] One must examine the extent to which the sterilized and the nonsterilized differ according to these key variables.

The first task is to construct current trends in sterilization across categories of the relevant variables. Estimates of this kind have been attempted in earlier works, some of which were previously cited. A principal shortcoming common to most of those efforts has been the lack of representative data. Given the availability of the national data and the importance of the task, an examination of these rates is the crucial and appropriate starting point.

Results

The rates presented are determined by dividing the number of women in a particular group who have been sterilized by the number of women in that group considered to be "at risk" for pregnancy. These rates will be expressed in sterilizations per 1,000 women. For the purposes of this study, the at-risk population includes all women not pregnant, trying to become pregnant, postpartum, menopausal, or noncontraceptively sterile. The assumption that if the male has had a vasectomy or is otherwise infertile then the woman is no longer at risk is met only when there is no premarital sex, when all marriages last until the woman dies or becomes infertile, and when fidelity is total. Given what is known about the rates of premarital sex, separation, divorce, re-marriage, and extra-marital sex (as described in Chapter 7), this assumption, which is taken for granted in all studies familiar to this author, is ludicrous. The at-risk definition includes only women for another important reason. The element of voluntarism is foremost in vasectomy—men must walk into a facility and ask for the operation. Female sterilization, on the other hand, occurs in an entirely different context and, as a procedure, can be subject to more institutional pressures. Women give birth in a strange, captive environment. Abortions are a particularly stressful decision. Women, during childbirth and abortion, are more susceptible to institutional and professional manipulation.[3] As Table 4-1 indicates, sterilization is performed infrequently on women with fewer than three children; therefore, much of our analysis will focus on women who have had three or more live births.

As shown in Table 4-1, the likelihood of sterilization tends to in-

TABLE 4-1
Cumulative Sterilization Rates (per 1,000), Selected Subgroups, 1976

		Chi Sq	dF	P=
Number of Live Births				
0	4			
1	15			
2	119			
3	181			
4+	302	820.814	4	.000
Race				
White	111			
Minority	115	.136	1	.711
Poverty Status				
<150% poverty level	167			
≥150% poverty level	94	58.484	1	.000
Welfare Status				
Recipient	188			
Nonrecipient	126	48.712	1	.000

Source: Shapiro, Fisher, and Diana 1983.

crease with the number of children a woman has had. Pronounced differences are also visible along poverty and welfare dimensions. Overall rates for whites and minorities are virtually identical, 111 to 115 per 1,000.

To allow for a fuller exploration of the racial and class or welfare-related dimensions, Table 4-2 examines sterilization rates by race and welfare status. Sterilization rates increase generally with age and level of parity; for those receiving welfare; and for those below the poverty line. Consistent with Table 4-1, those receiving public assistance have significantly higher rates of sterilization than those not receiving assistance. This developing pattern is consistent for women with more than one child, white and minority women, poor and non-poor women, and women older than twenty-four. However, within levels of parity, age, poverty status and welfare status, there is no consistent pattern or direction indicating support for a racial thesis.

TABLE 4-2

Sterilization Rates (per 1,000) by Race and Welfare Status, 1976

	Race		Welfare Status	
	Minority	*White*	*Recipient*	*Nonrecipient*
Number of Live Births				
0	6	4	—	—
1	3	19*	11	16
2	77	128[†]	125	115
3	185	183	260	173[§]
4+	307	303	433	274[#]
Race				
White	—	—	220	130[∥]
Minority	—	—	160	110**
Poverty Status				
<150% poverty level	150	181	203	166
≥150% poverty level	86	96	133	120
Welfare Status				
Recipient	160	220[‡]	—	—
Nonrecipient	110	130	—	—
Age				
15–24	25	27	42	43
25–34	128	117	224	125[††]
≥35	192	166	371	161[‡‡]

Source: Shapiro, Fisher, and Diana 1983.
* Chi Sq = 4.21; dF = 1; P = 0.4.   [#] Chi Sq = 20.60; dF = 1; P = .00.
[†] Chi Sq = 6.98; dF = 1; P = .008.   [∥] Chi Sq = 25.41; dF = 1; P = .00.
[‡] Chi Sq = 4.56; dF = 1; P = .03.   ** Chi Sq = 5.83; dF = 1; P = .01.
[§] Chi Sq = 5.83; dF = 1; P = .01   [††] Chi Sq = 25.30; dF = 1; P = .00.
                                          [‡‡] Chi Sq = 49.83; dF = 1; P = .00.

Rates of sterilization for whites and minorities are further presented in Table 4-3, which examines sterilization rates for women with three or more children. The trend observed suggests that minorities are only minimally more likely to be sterilized than whites, 256 per 1,000 versus 237. It is important to emphasize that these rates represent the cumulative pattern of sterilization for the cohort interviewed in Cycle II of the NSFG. While the comparison of white and

TABLE 4-3

Sterilization Rates (per 1,000) for Selected Subgroups in At-Risk Population Having Three or More Live Births, 1976

		Chi Sq	dF	P=
Race				
White	237			
Minority	256	.6785	1	.4101
Poverty Status				
<150% poverty level	304			
≥150% poverty level	209	20.9625	1	.0000
Welfare Status				
Recipient	366			
Nonrecipient	219	35.809	1	.0000

Source: Shapiro, Fisher, and Diana 1983. ˅

minority rates suggests that, on the whole, minorities are not disproportionately likely to be sterilized, these figures mask the information that minorities, until recently, were sterilized in substantially greater proportions than whites (Center for Disease Control 1979).

Table 4-4, based on Cycle I of the NSFG, compares minority and white sterilization rates (for those having three or more children in 1973) from 1968 to 1973 with those for the twelve months preceding the collection of Cycle II data (April 1975 to April 1976). As the table suggests, the cumulative pattern in Table 4-3 is caused by what had been a disproportionately low white sterilization rate increasing, to equal the continuing high rate for minorities.

While evidence of current racial bias in sterilization rates is not forthcoming from these data, the rates in Table 4-3 show that there are significant differences in incidence of sterilization along income and welfare lines. Those at risk whose incomes are below 150 percent of the poverty level are significantly more likely to be sterilized than those above that level, 304 per 1,000 versus 209. Moreover, a similar though slightly more pronounced trend is noted when rates for those in at-risk groups who receive welfare are compared with

TABLE 4-4

Comparison of Sterilization Rates (per 1,000) for Whites and
Nonwhites with Three or More Live Births Cumulative to 1973,
April 1975 to April 1976, and Cumulative to 1976

Race	Cumulative to 1973	Single Year Only 1975–1976	Cumulative to 1976
White	189	37	237
Minority	246*	51	256

Source: Shapiro, Fisher, and Diana 1983.
*Chi Sq = 10.4; dF = 1; P = .0012.

those for nonrecipients, 366 per 1,000 for recipients versus 219 for
nonrecipients. In a later phase of analysis, the interrelatedness of
poverty, race, and welfare will be sorted out. The rates shown here
are, nevertheless, the first strong, empirically based evidence indicating that the poor are sterilized at disproportionately higher rates.
The differentials for welfare and poor women are systematic and can
not be brushed aside. Rates for women receiving public assistance
with three or more children are 67 percent higher than for women not
on welfare with the same number of children; similarly, rates are 45
percent higher for poor versus nonpoor women with three or more
children. If nothing else, there is compelling, albeit preliminary, evidence that differential rates of sterilization exist. Findings suggest
that a type of population control exists, but not as argued in literature. In the data analyzed, the differential results are not as directly
racially based as they are class- and welfare-related; this finding will
be examined in a subsequent chapter.

In addition, studies based on 1980 Medicaid figures corroborate
the pervasiveness and the enduring nature of the pattern disclosed by
the NSFG. A report by the Health Care Financing Administration on
sterilization financed by Medicaid between 1976 and 1980 reveals
that women receiving Medicaid have a much higher rate of sterilization than women in the general population. The ratio of Medicaid
women to women in the general population undergoing sterilization

was 2.33 (Gerzowski et al. 1981). In all, 84,000 sterilizations were paid for by Medicaid in 1980, which is about 15 percent of the total, and 98 percent of those were performed on women. While the Medicaid data are raw figures, they indicate that the differential pattern has solidified and perhaps even deepened since 1976.

There are a number of possible differing interpretations for what might cause a pattern of differential sterilization outcomes. Population control is only one of several contending explanations. Literature on the placement and intent of family-planning clinics will be useful in constructing a framework of competing explanations to guide an interpretation. It involves one of those debates invested with enormous emotional fervor, but blessed with little reliable data. If one uses contraceptive sterilization as a test of these competing explanations, then the data should be consistent with some and inconsistent with others. The *fertility* thesis holds that levels of sterilization will be positively related to fertility levels found in the population (Kammeyer et al. 1975). As parity·increases, the proportion of women who have all the children they want increases. Consequently, in response to the greater risk of unwanted fertility, it is logical to expect that sterilization rates will increase with higher parity. Since the poor have larger families, it is logical for them to have higher rates of sterilization. This incorporates an assumption of equality in that sterilizations are directly related to the number of children, irrespective of class, welfare status, or race. The likelihood of sterilization, as shown in Table 4-1, increases with parity. There is support, and intuitive logic, for the basic proposition that sterilization is used principally where high levels of parity already exist.

An *altruistic* interpretation stipulates that sterilizations represent a desired or wanted service (Hout 1979; Wright 1978). According to this view, as the desire for sterilization varies across socioeconomic status, so too will rates of sterilization. Policy makers are responding to needs expressed by the community. Simply put, the poor and those on welfare have higher rates of sterilization because a greater proportion of them want to be sterilized. This sounds plausible and logical for the observed trend, but close inspection reveals the contrary. This interpretation was more closely scrutinized by profiling the distribution of women across the categories of race, poverty, and welfare who had not been sterilized (as opposed to the at-risk group) but who, at the time of the interview, planned to undergo sterilization after they attained their desired family size (these women are called *planners*). This profile can be compared to actual rates of sterilization and to the total sterilized within twelve months of the interview. If the altruistic hypothesis is correct, comparisons between planners and those actually sterilized should look similar. The profile of planners compared to those sterilized within twelve months are fairly similar across categories of race, poverty, and welfare. There are a few surprises in Table 4-5, however. White women plan to be sterilized at higher rates than nonwhite women, but nonwhites are actually sterilized at higher rates for the 1975–76 period (the numbers are not significant in either case). The tendency to plan a sterilization is minimally higher for those below than for those above 150 percent of poverty level. Actual sterilization rates are also higher, although the differences become more pronounced. Similarly, welfare recipients plan to be sterilized at higher rates than nonrecipients; indeed, more welfare clients in the at-risk group are sterilized. But while recipients *plan* to be sterilized at a rate that is 38 percent higher, their *actual rate* for the one year period is 91 percent higher. These differentials are further highlighted when one contrasts future plans against the cumulative rate, as shown in Table 4-3, where both poverty status and welfare are statistically significant. This paradox could suggest either that welfare clients independently consider sterilization a more viable option or that sterilizations are being offered more aggressively to them. Thus, while a more controlled analysis will be helpful, plans and outcomes do not go hand in hand positively across socioeconomic groups, thus casting serious doubt on the altruistic argument.

The *racial* hypothesis, a variant of the population-control theme, proposes that sterilization rates will be greater for racial and ethnic minorities (Darity et al. 1971). As previously shown, no trend indicated a positive correlation between race and sterilizations per se, but several facts must be noted before one rejects this notion. Sterilization among minorities has not declined. Instead, sterilizations

TABLE 4-5

Rates (per 1,000) of Planned and Actual Sterilization by Subgroups for April 1975 to April 1976

	Planned*	*Actual[†]*
Race		
White	215	37
Minority	209	51
Poverty Status		
<150% poverty level	222	57
≥150% poverty level	213	34
Welfare Status		
Recipient	260[‡]	67[§]
Nonrecipient	189	35

Source: Shapiro, Fisher, and Diana 1983.

* For general population.

[†] For those with three or more live births.

[‡] Chi Sq = 14.3538; dF = 1; P = .0001.

[§] Chi Sq = 4.745; dF = 1; P = .02.

among whites are increasing at a rate fast enough to have equalized earlier imbalances. Previous studies, including the 1973 NSFG, indicate that minority-white differentials were greater in earlier years (Center for Disease Control 1979). The closing of this gap can be construed in different ways. Those concerned about the racial thesis could point out that sterilization must occur only once to have a cumulative impact, hence a decrease in the minority-white gap is no cause for a celebration of equality. Furthermore, the "catch-up" appears to come among poorer whites on welfare.

The *poverty/class/welfare* thesis holds that sterilization will be related to socioeconomic levels. Mechanisms of social policy will structure choices and induce poorer people to opt for sterilization to curtail their fertility. A class based population control notion is embodied in this thesis. Differences are consistent and statistically significant: 49 percent higher for recipients versus nonrecipients; for women with three or more children, welfare recipients are sterilized at a rate that is 67 percent higher. Welfare status, regardless of race, appears to be a key dynamic. For instance, while the overall sterilization rate for the whole sample is 111, for white women on welfare it nearly doubles to 220. Any explanation of family-planning and sterilization policies must take this important finding into account.

Competing hypotheses, thus far, have been addressed by examining aggregate trends in sterilization and sterilization plans across categories of relevant variables. Because these variables are known to be interrelated, the need to examine each of these relationships while controlling effects of other variables has been stressed. Multivariate analysis is required, for instance, to isolate the effects of race from other possible correlating and confounding variables like class. This is accomplished through the use of maximum likelihood logistic regression, a multivariate technique appropriate for analysis involving binary dependent variables and a mix of categorical and continuous predictors, as is the case in the analysis developed here. The first of these regressions examines the effect of minority group status, poverty status, parity, and welfare status on planning to become sterilized (after desired family size is reached).[4] The results of this regression, shown in Table 4-6, are consistent with the findings of the

TABLE 4-6
Logistic Regression of "Plan to Be Sterilized" on Sociodemographic and Socioeconomic Factors in At-Risk Population

Predictor	Coefficient	t
Nonwhite Race	.015	.308*
Income ≤ 150% of poverty	.069	1.424*
Parity	−.375	−10.224[†]
Welfare status	.154	2.630[‡]
(Constant)	−.237	

Source: Shapiro, Fisher, and Diana 1983.

* Not significant

[†] P < .0005 (one-tailed test).

[‡] P < .005 (one-tailed test).

Goodness-of-fit Chi Sq = 51.728; dF = 27; P = .003; N = 4,651.

TABLE 4-7

Logistic Regression of Sterilization Outcome on Sociodemographic and Socioeconomic Factors for Women with Three or More Live Births

Predictor	Coefficient	t
Nonwhite Race	−.179	−2.462*
Income ≤150% of poverty	.162	2.440*
Parity	.567	5.170[†]
Welfare status	.231	2.849[‡]
(Constant)	−3.055	

Source: Shapiro, Fisher, and Diana 1983.

* P < .01 (one-tailed test).
[†] P < .0005 (one-tailed test).
[‡] P < .005 (one-tailed test).

Goodness-of-fit Chi Sq = 20.427; dF = 11; P = .040; N = 1,990.

tabular analysis. No significant relationship between plans to be sterilized and minority-group membership was found, which is consistent with earlier analysis. Also compatible with the tabular analysis is the finding that poverty status alone appears to have little impact. In the regression analysis, welfare status has a significant effect on the likelihood of planning to be sterilized (p < .005). In addition, a somewhat paradoxical but highly significant negative relationship between parity and the likelihood of planning a sterilization was observed.

The second logistic regression examines the dependent variable measuring whether or not a woman has actually had a sterilization with the same set of explanatory variables used to predict plans. These results, estimated for that portion of the sample having three or more live births, are presented in Table 4-7. Examination of these regression coefficients confirms the results of the tabular analysis.[5] All the independent variables are significant predictors of the probability of being sterilized, and all, with the exception of race, are in the expected direction. Welfare status, next to parity, is again the most powerful positive predictor of the likelihood of one's being sterilized, here controlling for poverty and minority-group membership.

This suggests, once more, that selection of the sterilization option might be more actively pursued for those on welfare. Race is also significant, but it is positive for whites, not minorities. Furthermore, welfare status is a stronger predictor on actual sterilization than on plans.

Of additional interest is the finding that live births exceeding three were positively associated with becoming sterilized. This effect, which is stronger than that of other variables, is consistent with the fertility hypothesis. When the effect of this variable in the equation is compared to that in the "plans" equation, a paradox is noted: women having high levels of parity appear less likely to plan to become sterilized. However, the greater the number of births over three, the greater is the likelihood that the mother will be sterilized.

Since 1971, a period during which general reduction of programs and services had occurred for poor people, sterilization services have increased for them at the highest rates. While there is an expressed desire for birth control and maternal-related services among the poor (Blake 1975b; *Family Planning Digest* 1972b), there is absolutely no evidence that the poor or women on welfare are clamoring for sterilization. In the process of delivering publicly assisted family-planning health care, services are channeled toward those that are permanent.

Summary

The data sustained the fertility argument along with the poverty/ class/welfare thesis. The fertility notion uses an assumption of equality: fertility levels should be the primary correlate of sterilization— extraneous social factors need not be invoked. Logically, except for esoteric reasons, demand for sterilization generally should be linked to fulfillment of ideal family size. Data are consistent with this idea, but it is not the only theory supported by evidence. Systematic differentials remain, even when controlling for parity. The other supported thesis, on the contrary, uses an assumption of inequality. The data sustained fertility and population-control arguments; this may reflect the complex, subtle nature of inequality in American society.

Abuses, often flagrant, were widespread between 1970 to 1976. Since 1974, partially due to federal regulations and the sensitivity they produced, reports of glaring abuses have diminished. However, hospitals and doctors have not complied fully with existing regulations. The pattern of who is sterilized is slanted systematically toward the poor and those on welfare. Differentials are real and can not be brushed aside by the competing interpretations, all of which except the fertility argument, empirically fall short of explaining why there are consistent differences in female sterilization.

To comprehend why this discriminatory pattern exists, one must analyze the deeper social, economic, and cultural roots from which the statistical dimension springs. The next chapter examines why poor women on welfare have higher rates of sterilization.

NOTES

1. The findings presented are from an article by Shapiro, Fisher, and Diana (1983). I want to acknowledge the valuable contributions by my co-authors, William Fisher and Augusto Diana.
2. The data collection procedure used a multistage probability sample, in which blacks were oversampled. To compensate for this and other biases, a complex weighting scheme was used to arrive at a post-stratified weight, the use of which allows unbiased estimation of population parameters.

The National Center for Health Statistics uses over 1500 separate weighting factors to develop a mean post-stratified weighting value, which can then be applied to the sample to obtain unbiased estimates of the population. A comprehensive discussion of this weighting scheme can be found in the documentation accompanying the National Survey of Family Growth, Cycle II (National Center for Health Statistics 1979). The multivariate analysis presented here was performed on a data set weighted differently from that used in the tabular analysis. This weighting, necessitated by the computer algorithm used to perform the logistic regression analysis, did not substantially alter either the total sample size or the relative proportions of individuals in categories of the variables used in the analysis. One can thus assume that results are not biased by this reweighting.

In this analysis, race is examined by looking at whites and minorities (blacks and Hispanics). Poverty status, a computer-generated variable, was calculated by dividing total family income by the weighted average threshold income of nonfarm families (head of household, under sixty-five); this was based on poverty levels in the U.S. Bureau Of Census Current Population Reports, P-60, "Money Income in 1975 of Families and Persons in the U.S.," table A-3. The 1976 Poverty Index centered around an annual family income of $5,815 for a nonfarm family of four; thus 150 percent of poverty implies an average family income of $8,723 (Ford 1978). The cutoff point of 150 percent is suggested and justified in Cutright and Jaffe (1977). Welfare status is indicated by receipt of either AFDC or Medicaid payments. Parity is the number of children in the household.

3. Defining "at risk" is conceptually perilous because it involves a choice of two mutually exclusive assumptions, neither of which is totally satisfactory. Biases are inherent in both. Previous examinations of sterilization assume that if the husband is contraceptively sterile, his spouse is not at risk to become pregnant. Given present levels of separation, divorce, remarriage, single parenthood, and extramarital sexual relations (which will be statistically described in Chapter 7), women whose husbands are sterilized are still "at risk" to become pregnant. Moreover, vasectomies occur most frequently among white, middle-class men. Incorporating this assumption would have the artificial impact of narrowing any class- or welfare-related differences in the delivery of reproductive health and family-planning services. For example, 98 percent of Medicaid-financed sterilizations in 1980 were performed on women (Gerzowski et al. 1981).

The opposite assumption—that a women is still at risk even if her husband is sterilized—has built-in biases. Moral assumptions aside, in either case the woman can become pregnant, thus both assumptions have flaws. This definition of "at risk" is confined to women. This reversal of the usual assumption is justifiable and appropriate for several reasons. Federally financed clinics service a population that is primarily female. The concern here is to investigate whether sterilization differentials exist and, if so, to begin locating the source of any differences. Neither of the at-risk assumptions is flawless; thus one must adopt a definition that gives the fullest picture of female reproductive health care.

4. Variables were coded in the following manner: minority group status (1 = nonwhite, 0 = white); poverty status (1 = less than 150 percent of poverty, 0 = above); welfare status (1 = receiving AFDC or Medicaid, 0 = not); plans to be sterilized (1 = yes, 0 = no); and actual sterilization (1 = sterilized, 0 = not).

5. The obvious interrelatedness of these variables, particularly poverty and welfare status (whose zero-order correlations were .47 in the total sample and .48 in the sample with three or more live births), raises issues of possible multicollinearity. However, an examination of correlations between logistic regression coefficients, a reliable check on multicollinearity, showed little evidence of linear dependence among the predictors.

5
The Roots of Discriminatory Sterilization

THIS CHAPTER explores the permeation of a population-control perspective into different layers of contemporary society. How much of the discriminatory sterilization pattern can be attributed to individual, institutional, or societal embracing of population-control objectives? The dynamic encompasses doctors, hospitals, family-planning personnel, and street-level welfare bureaucrats, as well as social policy. It is appropriate, too, to explore and gauge the impact of public policy in this area.

This chapter examines the following proposition for women on welfare. Typically, sterilization is neither actively coerced by public institutions nor voluntarily proposed as the client's preference. Rather, the choice emerges from the deeply ingrained nature of population control in American culture, the attitudes and practices of the medical profession toward women and welfare clients, the dynamics of social policy, the range of and access to available family-planning services, and the structural receptivity of agencies delivering public family-planning services to cost- and time-efficient methods of permanent fertility control.

A complete turnabout from private vice to public virtue characterizes the nation's attitude toward federally sponsored family-planning services. Dwight Eisenhower, former U.S. president, solemnly declared that "birth control . . . is not our business." He could not imagine "anything more emphatically a subject that is not a proper political or governmental activity" (Piotrow 1973, x). The nation's changing attitude, like the much-heralded sexual revolution of the 1960s, was accompanied by turbulence. How much attitudes have changed can be measured by past resistance to birth control, especially the pill. One Massachusetts legislator, William X. Wall, exclaimed in horror: "No way should this be allowed. If she's gonna play, she's gonna pay" (McLaughlin 1983, 12).

The Office of Economic Opportunity (OEO) was established to wage the war on poverty, and it was the first public agency to offer family-planning services to the poor. Initially, however, only married women living with their spouses were eligible, and sterilizations were strictly prohibited. Abortions, which were illegal at the time, were not offered. In the mid-1960s, the first OEO project grant for direct family-planning services was awarded. More important, in 1967 provisions of the Social Security Act governing Aid to Families with Dependent Children (AFDC) were revised to earmark at least 6 percent of maternal- and infant-care monies for family-planning assistance. Since 1975, amendments to Title XIX (Medicaid) and Title IV-A (AFDC) of the Social Security Act stipulate that the federal government will reimburse 90 percent of the state expenses to "all current and potential recipients of AFDC." States are required to provide services to all Medicaid clients who want them and to provide such services "promptly" to all current AFDC clients of child-bearing age. Many states choose to offer family-planning services to "potential" clients (Family Planning Digest 1974a, 2). The act also offers matching federal funds for all family-planning services, giving the federal government leverage to set levels of future services. Opponents of welfare, especially AFDC, made their support of welfare contingent upon an activist line of family planning, not as much out of humane concerns as for reasons of cutting future welfare costs (Piotrow 1973).

Most significant of all, Congress in 1970 passed the Family Planning Services and Population Research Act, the first legislation dealing exclusively with family planning, and sought eventually to provide services to all poor women. Five million women were targeted as women in need of family-planning services, yet receiving none; this figure expanded each year so that by 1980 the targeted clientele had doubled to 9.9 million women (U.S. Department of Health and Human Services 1980). Public family-planning programs were not part of a broad package of health services for the needy; instead, these programs were isolated from general health care.

Family-planning clinics have grown substantially since federal funds to support these services became available. In 1965, at the outset of commitment to public funding, 450,000 individuals were serviced by existing public programs; by 1975 the programs had grown eightfold to more than 3.8 million; and by 1979 the clinics were seeing 4.5 million women. This heady growth was stimulated by government's rhetorical and financial commitment to deliver family-planning services to the poor. Between fiscal years 1965 and 1979 federal monies for family planning grew from less than $5 million to more than $260 million. Some programs offer free services while others charge fees that cover all or part of the cost. Virtually all patients have low or marginal incomes (Jaffe 1974; U.S. Department of Health and Human Services 1980).

The Guideline Snafu

In 1969, the assistant director of OEO, Frank Carlucci, sought to make sterilization a part of OEO family-planning progams, but Donald Rumsfeld, the more politically oriented director, refused to sign the order (Littlewood 1977). In 1971, after the family-planning constituency lobbied for a change and some 80 percent of OEO projects around the country expressed a desire to add sterilization to their services, the first sanctioned OEO use of sterilization occurred when OEO approved grant monies (*Medical World News* 1973). Carlucci was then the boss at OEO; yet, even then, OEO-funded family-planning clinics were asked to withhold sterilizations until a set of guidelines could be issued (U.S. Senate Subcommittee on Health 1973). However, sterilizations had been performed before 1971 under the auspices of Medicaid and other government programs. The guidelines drafted by OEO were not released until 1974, a period during which several hundred thousand sterilizations—and the most blatant abuses—took place (U.S. Subcommittee on Health 1973). Flagrant cases of abuse, such as that of the Relf sisters, might have been prevented if guidelines had been issued promptly..

In May 1971 OEO issued a memorandum to its regional directors announcing a change in policy to permit payments for sterilization. The memo contained the following request: "Please do not consider any funding requests for sterilization services until you receive . . . guidelines" (U.S. Senate Subcommittee on Health 1973). Regulations were being prepared because, as one journalistic investigation termed it, there was "no wish to allow OEO-funded sterilization to run on unguided" (*Medical World News* 1973, 54). OEO officials drafted a set of guidelines within a few months. In January 1972, twenty-five thousand copies were printed for distribution to OEO projects. On February 2, 1972, a news conference announcing the long-awaited guidelines was scheduled, the press releases were written, and twenty-five thousand copies were ready for distribution. But the press conference was canceled, and the guidelines were not released; instead, they began to gather dust in a Washington warehouse. It took thirty-five months from the time of official OEO authorization, and twenty-seven months after they were originally printed, for the first safeguards to finally reach the field. Health, Education, and Welfare (HEW), under Caspar Weinberger, issued the first federal regulations (42 C.F.R. Section 50; 45 C.F.R. Section 205).

When the federal regulations were released, they barred the sterilization of minors and those who could not legally consent. A seventy-two hour waiting period between the signing of an informed consent form and the procedure was mandated. These guidelines applied to government-supported sterilizations only. In formulating these guidelines, OEO sought the assistance of the Association for Voluntary Sterilization (AVS), the American Public Health Association, Planned Parenthood, and the American College of Obstetricians and Gynecologists (ACOG). The guidelines, according to the deputy director of OEO, "quoted liberally from a report prepared for the Population Council. . . ." (U.S. Senate Subcommittee on Health 1973, 1516). These guidelines were ineffectual and unenforced.

The government wrote guidelines, printed them, and then suppressed them. It seems that conflicting bureaucratic and political pressures and intrabureaucratic politics produced Catch-22 results (*Medical World News* 1973, 54; Littlewood 1977; U.S. Senate Subcommittee on Health 1973). One group of public-health physicians lobbied to preclude flagrant abuses by federally funded agencies. Once the instructions were issued, sterilizations could proceed smoothly. Some of these physicians generated correspondence from the family-planning constituency across the country to urge release of the instructions (Littlewood 1977). Other public-health workers, sensitive to allegations of genocide from the black community, tried to forestall release because they feared undue emphasis on sterilization, to the exclusion of other family-planning methods.

White House intervention ultimately suppressed release of the regulations because 1972 was an election year, and the Nixon administration did not want to be connected to sterilization. White House action stemmed from concern about the reaction of its Roman Catholic constituency.

Ironically, during the internecine battle over guidelines, HEW had a flourishing but quiet sterilization operation financed through Medicaid and other family-planning programs. The upshot of this squabble was that approximately 100,000 sterilizations were financed annually, without the benefit of elementary safeguards— right up to the time the guidelines were finally released (*Relf v. Weinberger et al.* 1974).

Physician Attitudes and Welfare

Legislation encompassing population-control themes without safeguards matches traditional attitudes of the medical profession toward the poor and women. Two surveys of physicians' attitudes about family planning, at the time of the policy change, indicate a lack of confidence in the ability of poor people to use contraception effectively. They tended to favor punitive action, such as compulsory sterilization or withholding of support to welfare mothers. In one study, southern physicians were asked to differentiate between contraceptive methods for private and public patients: 6 percent chose sterilization as their first choice for private patients in contrast to 14 percent for public cases. Many physicians indicated that public patients were not sufficiently "reliable," "intelligent," or "motivated" to use contraception, such as the pill, effectively (Measham et al. 1971). Obstetrician-gynecologists were the most punitive of the doctors surveyed: 94 percent favored compulsory sterilization or the withholding of welfare for unwed mothers with three children. A 1971 study of northern physicians revealed a belief that women with low education or low income would be unreliable contraceptors: 30 percent said a woman should be taken off welfare if she did not agree to contraceptive sterilization after her third illegitimate child (Silver 1971).

Defining excessive childbearing among the poor as being deviant fits a recent trend toward medicalization of social problems, which allows for the exertion of medical social control (Conrad 1975). Social-economic conditions can then be treated as a "medical" indicator for sterilization, which allows practices that could otherwise not be considered; for example, consenting to sterilization becomes a precondition for abortion. This form of medical social control assumes that excessive childbearing is a medical problem. It requires that something is wrong with the woman—she can not count days, remember to take pills, or say no. There are solutions to such behavioral problems. Once labeled, the individual is expected to accept others' definitions of her behavioral problems. Physicians' attitudes toward the poor are related to their practices with female patients. It is well documented that women are more likely than men to undergo unnecessary elective surgery. The thesis that doctors take liberties with women may be unpalatable to some, yet there is ample published evidence that some doctors continue to persuade women to undergo unnecessarily dangerous procedures. Misogynist womb envy, as suggested by one female physician (Savage 1982), may express itself in an overeagerness to sterilize women. At a conference in 1969, one male physician lent credence to this when he said: "No ovary is good enough to leave in and no testicle is bad enough to take out" (cited in Gray 1974, 172). Traditional attitudes toward women and the poor are compatible with population-control objectives, and sterilization is one way this match is materialized. One physician expressed a belief in a kind of reproductive determinism—that contraception will raise a woman's standard of living—writing that he was "in complete agreement that poor women, be they black or Indian, will have little chance to escape from the poverty cycle if they do not have complete, unhampered access to fertility control" (*Medical Tribune* 1978). Another physician said that he pushes sterilization in his clinic in California because "it costs a lot of money to raise children. Those people make only about $8,000 a year, so you and I who pay taxes have to end up paying for it" (*Washington Star* 1980).

Physicians' attitudes toward the poor and women can arise from overt class and sex biases, but one can safely assume that doctors will apply the evaluations of social worth common to their culture (Roth 1974). Physicians may apply different practices, which are determined by whether patients are private, public, male, or female. In this perspective it would be surprising if poor women on welfare received the same treatment as everybody else. The remuneration, prestige, and psychic reward a physician receives are normally tied to the social composition of their clientele; this structuring of rewards underlies and reinforces differential treatment.

Medical insurance provides an avenue of structural receptivity and lucrative rewards for the training and practices of the medical profession. A survey of fertility-control coverage revealed coverage to be inadequate. Contraception is often ignored; despite improvements, abortion coverage is incomplete. Sterilization, not surprisingly, is covered well. Of the thirty-seven responding private health insurance companies, only one covered oral contraceptives or diaphragms and two covered intrauterine devices. Eleven companies did not include unmarried employees in their standard maternity packages; six did not cover wives of employees. In contrast, female sterilization is covered by thirty-four of the thirty-seven commercial carriers and is reimbursed according to regular fee schedules. Vasectomy is included by twenty-seven of the companies (Muller 1978). In 1983 abortion coverage was taken away from federal employees.

Historically, there has been a symbiosis between the medical profession and population control. Attitudes do translate into practice here, yet all the differences can not be explained by the presence of misogynist or welfare-hating doctors. Deeper, structural causes must be sought to explain such wide and persistent differences. Social policies function to formulate courses of action, choices, and priorities—usually on a macro level—to produce desired outcomes. The possibility that discriminatory sterilization results from social policy must be seriously considered, and it is appropriate to begin by further examining attitudes toward women on welfare.

Coercion against poor people has been based historically on a deeply ingrained attitude about their sexual behavior. Midnight visits, man-in-the-house laws, and myriad harassing control mechanisms were justified by the suspected illicit sexual relationships of welfare clients (Piven and Cloward 1971). Senator Russell B. Long said there is a "rising objection to people who lie about all day making love and producing illegitimate babies." He referred to poverty mothers and welfare advocates as "Black Brood Mares" (cited in Placek and Hendershot 1974, 658–59). The sentiment against welfare 'chiselers' in the 1960s was so strong that many states proposed compulsory sterilization for welfare mothers (Paul 1968).

This attitude illustrates a powerful Malthusian legacy that holds sway over welfare policy: the poor beget children to secure public welfare. The legacy is based on the assumption that poor women have more children than those who are better off and more responsible (W. Bell 1983); in reality, the difference amounts to about half a child. A common-sense liberal approach argues that the poor, therefore, must have access to contraceptive services. Indeed, family-planning services *must* be offered to welfare recipients.

Welfare issues became linked to environmental concerns in the 1970s. One influential advocate of population control (a former AVS president) linked the issues when he succinctly argued that "people pollute, and too many people crowded too close together cause many of our social and economic problems. These, in turn, are aggravated by involuntary and irresponsible parenthood." But there is hope because "the welfare mess, as it has been called, cries out for solution, one of which is fertility control" (Wood 1973, 39). The chairman of the Texas Board of Human Resources, which oversees the state's welfare agency, has urged mandatory sterilization of welfare recipients. As recently as 1980, he tersely declared: "I'm a little discouraged and irritated at the families growing in size all the time and those of us who work and pay taxes having to pay for them" (cited in Sigelman 1981, 22).

If one recognizes that poor people lack alternatives to seeking services through public programs, then the voluntary nature of their involvement becomes suspect. The alternative to voluntary family-planning services may be to neglect reproductive health altogether. If this is the case, then to call compliance a pure expression of choice is philosophically and practically illogical. Clients in public family-planning services may desire services, but their participation can not be considered voluntary; clinics supply essential services clients cannot obtain elsewhere, and they are under pressure to obtain family-planning services. Reproductive health care can be obtained privately, but only at relatively high costs. Private doctors are so costly, relative to income, that poor people are forced to seek assistance through public agencies or, worse yet, not to seek assistance at all. A relatively affluent woman has the freedom to choose a private physician instead of a public clinic, an option that is less available for the poor. The relationship between poor people and public agencies in general provides grounds for concluding that poor people receive a qualitatively different kind of treatment from the state (Lipsky 1980). Family-planning clinics and doctors usually have nothing to lose from failing to satisfy clients.

Data on sterilization patterns demonstrate that something in the dynamics of administering public family-planning and reproductive services has the effect of delivering qualitatively different treatment that results in much higher rates of sterilization. Thus far the explanation has focused on the attractiveness of population control to political, policy, and economic elites at the level of policy formation.

Population-control solutions also fit prevailing cultural attitudes about welfare clients and "proper" sexuality. Because reproductive health care and family-planning workers do not, as a rule, coerce or trick clients into being sterilized, public services must be examined for elements that produce systematic bias.

Michael Lipsky (1980) argues that the decisions of workers delivering public services, the routines they establish, and the devices they invent to cope with uncertainty and pressure become public policies. That is, the work conditions of "street-level bureaucrats" shape practices and services, which become public policy.

Family-planning workers are in a position to make policy with respect to significant aspects of their interactions with clients. Discretion and relative autonomy from organizational authority are the two largest facets of their policy-making roles; however, discretion and relative autonomy occur within policy contexts that are set by policy elites and political and administrative officials. For example, abortion is not a discretionary option. Within set boundaries family-planning workers exercise wide discretion about the choices they stress for their clients; they are usually free from direct supervision or accountability to the general public (much less their clients); and they often disregard client preference. Their routines warrant scrutiny because their clients' lives are deeply affected by family-planning decisions. Of all the services and benefits offered by the welfare state, sterilization is certainly among the most lasting.

Lipsky sees the problem of street-level bureaucrats in the following way: they attempt to do a good job, but it is impossible to do the job in ideal terms. Conditions of work shape their perception of problems and, in turn, help to frame solutions. Public-service work is characterized by a chronic shortage of resources, a demand for services that always seems to increase to meet supply, ambiguous or conflicting objectives, few controls, discouraging circumstances, and a nonvoluntary clientele. Street-level bureaucrats develop at least two methods of coping: (1) they develop patterns of practice that tend to limit demand and maximize the utilization of available resources, and (2) they modify their concept of clients so that the gap between accomplishment and objectives becomes more acceptable. The services they actually deliver add up to street-level policy.

Family-planning workers, by limiting clients' demands and maximizing the use of existing resources, can cope with difficult work circumstances in order to do the best job possible. From a crude bureaucratic-centered point of view, the most expedient and efficient form of birth control is sterilization, but this may conflict with client-centered human services. The preponderance of rewards for family-planning workers and clinics is heavily weighted toward more permanent options. The woman utilizing client-centered methods like birth-control pills consumes one of the most precious and under-supplied resources—time. In contrast, sterilized women make fewer demands on a worker's time. In an understaffed and underfunded agency, sterilization "frees" resources and theoretically cuts case loads. It is a way of coping with mass processing, case overloads, and "difficult" clients, as well as the ramifications of fiscal crisis and extreme cost-efficiency methods.

From the welfare client's viewpoint, these bureaucratic hassles may well have meaning for future decisions. For the welfare client who wants no more children, sterilization may seem an attractive alternative to busy, impersonal, degrading services. It eliminates repeated check-up appointments, travel, and, in some cases, personal expense for creams, jellies or pills. There may be pragmatic reasons for welfare clients to perceive sterilization as desirable—within the limited context of what is available and how they are treated—and thus to "choose" it.

There is a further dimension of how work conditions tend to structure incentives for the family-planning worker. Clients who become pregnant are a measure—formal and informal, conscious and unconscious—of the worker's performance. Regardless of how the worker socially constructs the client and her failure, a pregnancy is the most outward and obvious sign that the worker's counsel may have been inappropriate. Time and energy spent on a client who becomes pregnant were wasted, and the "failure" goes on to use more resources of the welfare state; thus the agency has failed to accomplish one of its primary objectives. Single women with children are a priori suspect in their ability to use contraception successfully. Methods that do not rely on the client's discretion—intrauterine devices, sterilization, or, possibly in the near future, Depo-Provera—are options more favorably structured by an internal system of incentives. There are few institutional disincentives for permanent or longer-lasting methods, whereas the work conditions of the bureaucracy structure important rewards for precisely those methods.

Budgetary priorities that underlie and structure bureaucratic pressures and work conditions are becoming intractable. While family-planning budgets have not been decimated like other public services, this welfare service is nonetheless caught up in similar dynamics. Lipsky maintains that in an inflationary era of constant fiscal crisis the budgetary convention is to ask the agency to maintain efforts on the basis of last year's allocation—while costs for goods, services, and salaries are increasing, thus insuring that resources will be chronically inadequate.

A second way family-planning workers cope with their job conditions is seen in how they socially construct their clients. This fundamental part of being a "helping professional" is initially learned in the process of training. There is a tendency in the helping professions in general, according to Lipsky, to blame the victim, attributing the cause of the client's situation to the individual irrespective of the role of social and environmental contexts. This identifies responsibility in a way that absolves the helpers from blame.

There is an opposite but fundamentally equivalent way of seeing clients that also deflects responsibility. This is the culture of poverty view that tends to "perceive clients exclusively as the products of inadequate background conditioning" (Lipsky 1980, 153). Thus if the welfare client is perceived as passive, a slave to passions, or unable to defer immediate gratification or take appropriate precautions, then family-planning workers can hardly fault themselves if contraception fails. In this view, as well as that of blaming the victim, permanent and drastic interventions are justified as being in the client's best interest. These views reverberate among other workers who work in a structure that tends to confirm their biases and thus reproduce them in street-level practices.

Lipsky points out that "unsanctioned, persistent differentiation is supported by the cultural attitudes and prejudices that permeate the society and are grounded in the structure of inequality" (Lipsky 1980, 115). While differentiation is intrinsic to street-level bureaucracies, social inequality allows it to continue. The need to routinize, conserve resources, simplify, and differentiate in the context of inequality leads to the institutionalization of the stereotypical tendencies that permeate society. Whatever prejudices family-planning workers as individuals do or do not have, the structure of their work calls for differentiation of the client population—thus there is structural receptivity to prejudicial attitudes.

The problem of institutionalized discrimination is profound, not only for the inferior quality of services to the poor but also for the legitimacy of government. There can be little official recognition of institutionalized discrimination if it serves the ends of policy elites and is bureaucratically functional.

Practices that arise from the way family-planning workers cope with difficult work situations appear to be consistent with the objective and interests of population control. The links between social policy and public-service practice are not direct, but they are easy to discern and apparently have no intractable conflict between them. There are striking parallels in the population controller's solution of conserving precious resources by limiting the growth of demand and the way in which family-planning bureaucracies act to stretch available resources. Indeed, as shall be seen in more detail, policy analysts and administrative officials justify family-planning services on a cost-benefit basis: allocating certain services now will save potential welfare costs later. The more permanent the service, the surer and greater will be the future saving. To be sure, the meaning of doing a good job is quite different for the family-planning worker and the efficiency-conscious official. The dynamics of public family-planning intrinsically reward population-control solutions despite the idealism that workers bring to their jobs. Family-planning workers, however, become less idealistic, and some become bitter and angry about their clients' behavior. Family-planning workers are among the large group of lowly paid, salaried workers who are subjected to the regressive tax structure. The view that welfare mothers are a tax burden seems to find grounding in family-planning workers' material reality. Therefore, class biases of population control are intertwined with political priorities and rooted in bureaucratic practices and priorities.

Social Policy

Doctors' attitudes, cultural attitudes toward welfare, and the dynamics of delivering public family planning services complement broader social policy, which functions to channel these services in a subtle yet effective manner. Social policy shapes the pattern of family-planning services for welfare recipients by structuring a positive institutional receptivity toward long-lasting methods while discouraging or refusing access to alternative methods. Since 1975, under revisions to Section XIX (Medicaid) of the Social Security Act, the federal government has provided 90 percent of the cost of sterilizing poor or medically indigent clients. At the same time, abortion, which was then legal and government supported, was being reimbursed at 50 percent. Enacted in a time of rising inflation, swelling unemployment, reduced standards of living, and political retrenchment, the 1975 revisions give health-care agencies economic incentive to persuade Medicaid patients to choose sterilization. Ninety-percent funding offers a powerful, seductive inducement to clinics, doctors, and hospitals to promote a service they are committed to provide.

There are good reasons to believe that the 90–50 percent differential represents a strategy. The editors of *Family Planning Digest*, the official HEW family-planning publication, prophetically hoped in 1972 to "see sterilization become as important in family planning in the fifty states as it already is in Puerto Rico" (Family Planning Digest 1972a, 4).

Rosie Jimenez died from an illegal, unsafe abortion. The same government that would have paid to sterilize the twenty-seven year-old Chicana woman living with her young daughter in Texas had decided in 1977 to withhold funds that would have helped her obtain a safe abortion. The death of Rosie Jimenez was the first to be reported as a result of the 1977 Hyde Amendment, which cut off Medicaid funds for abortion. When federal monies for abortion were barred, indigent women were left with a choice of paying for an abortion or "choosing" a nearly free sterilization. Within rational economic decision making the choices are so heavily weighted as to consist of a de facto policy of sterilization.

Until 1977 Medicaid paid the substantial share of the cost of abortion for poor women. In each of the next several years, with the encouragement of Presidents Carter and Reagan and the endorsements of the U.S. Supreme Court, Congress added restrictions until finally federal funds for abortion could be used only when a woman's life was endangered, thereby excluding pregnancy that resulted from rape or incest. Denying poor women access to abortions apparently became de facto national policy. This caused the number of abortions partly financed by federal funds to drop from 300,000 in 1977 to 17,983 in 1981. Some states, like New York, compensated for this law by appropriating funds for abortion (W. Bell 1983). Petchesky reports that an "estimated *94 percent of Medicaid-dependent women needing abortions continued to get them*" (Petchesky 1984, 160). Congressional action and right-wing pressure have not stopped abortion, but have altered the social conditions under which it occurs. The long-range impact may be different and remains to be seen. Data reveal that Medicaid sterilizations for women rose sharply by 30.4 percent between 1977 and 1981. This is no mere coincidence because privately financed sterilizations for women actually declined by 14.7 percent between 1977 and 1981 (Gerzowski et al. 1981).

Finally, in terms of social policy, one must remember that family-planning clinics are isolated from other forms of health care, all of which are less accessible to the poor than reproductive health care. One must also question why sterilization in the face of a fiscal crisis, is more accessible and cost-free than other services for the poor, which in reality are diminishing. Social policy shapes behavior not only by the services it provides, but also by the services it does not offer. In their 1973 letter to HEW Secretary Weinberger, which raised doubts about the voluntary family-planning programs, especially sterilization, for minorities, black Congresswomen Chisholm, Burke, Jordan, and Collins also captured the irony of a sudden diffusion of government-sponsored family-planning programs: "A few years ago social service recipients could not secure information on birth control if they got down on their knees and begged for it. Today welfare case workers and other social service workers in the field are sometimes zealous to the point of being pushy" (U.S. Senate Subcommittee on Health 1973, 1562–63)

Impact of Policy and Practices

It is vital to have some indication of the impact of these policies on family planning and sterilization. Have the policies affected (1) the pattern of sterilization, (2) welfare costs, and (3) the fertility rates of the poor? If so, is it possible to enumerate the various consequences? To gauge the practical effects of a population policy emphasizing the most permanent methods, it is necessary to examine these three areas. The projections required to make these estimates are hampered mainly by a lack of comparative data, sometimes by imprecise procedures, and occasionally by extrapolations from different data bases. The results, therefore, are intended to be illustrative and should in no way be regarded as definitive.

The first potential impact to examine is whether the general sterilization pattern has changed since the inception of federal family-planning programs and infusion of federal monies (1965), and since sterilization was officially authorized (1971). Were class-based differences already present, both in preference and in actual prevalence? Comparing sterilization patterns for 1965 and 1976 ideally would produce the most pertinent information. Choosing 1965 as the baseline year is an appropriate anchor because it best allows for an approximation of a before-after model, the important difference being the added availability of sterilization amidst a setting of public family-planning services. Bumpass and Presser (1972) provide the

TABLE 5-1
Positive Attitude toward Sterilization: 1965 and 1970

Family Income	Percent Approving			
	1965		*1970*	
	Male	*Female*	*Male*	*Female*
≤ $ 5,000	30	37	42	48
5,000–6,999	32	36	45	50
7,000–9,999	33	36	47	49
≥ 10,000	39	42	57	58

Source: Bumpass and Presser 1972.

only thorough and meticulous analysis of sterilization for this earlier period. Variations in populations sampled and differences in variables under scrutiny, however, create limitations for direct comparisons. Their study is based on responses from the National Fertility Study (NFS), which focuses on women currently married and living with their spouse. While comparisons between the limited NFS sample and the more representative National Survey of Family Growth (NSFG) sample must be approached with caution, such comparisons do supply the needed reference points for both attitudes about and prevalence of sterilization in 1965.

Table 5-1 shows that favorable attitudes toward sterilization dramatically increase for everybody sampled between 1965 and 1970. There is a correlation between income levels and approval: the most favorable attitudes are found at the highest income levels. Even though general approval of sterilization increases with income, the actual prevalence does not, and this is especially true of female sterilization. Pertinent information is given in Table 5-2, which shows the prevalence of female sterilization for various income groups in 1965. Among those eligible for public assistance, roughly those under $5,000, the rate is slightly higher. Some of the difference, as with NSFG data, occurs because higher-income couples are more likely to opt for vasectomy.

TABLE 5-2

Prevalence of Female Sterilization: 1965

Family Income	
≤ $ 5,000	8%
5,000–6,999	6%
7,000–9,999	5%
≥ 10,000	6%

Source: Bumpass and Presser 1972.

TABLE 5-3

Prevalence of Female Sterilization

	1965	1976	Increase (from 1965–1976)
Poverty status	8%	16.7%	109%
Nonpoverty	6%	9.4%	57%
Welfare	—	18.8%	
Nonwelfare	—	12.6%	

Source: Bumpass and Presser 1972; and original data.

Comparing sterilization in 1965 and 1976, as displayed in Table 5-3, provides a rough indicator of how the general sterilization pattern has changed since federal intervention. The rate of increase for the poor is nearly twice that of the nonpoor: 108 percent versus 57 percent. The differentials in prevalence among those eligible for public assistance, while apparent yet minimal in 1965, widen dramatically by 1976. Since federal programs have been inaugurated the overall pattern of sterilization has changed.

Estimating the second potential consequence, that of welfare cost cutting, also entails the use of projections. To determine the impact of family planning generally, or sterilization specifically, one must estimate the costs and benefits of public family-planning programs. Previous cost-benefit analyses have calculated the long-term benefits of family-planning programs by projecting the number of births averted by such services, the cost of delivering those services, and the expenditure needed to rear a child to adulthood. Obviously such measures are crude, materialistic ratios that do not allow for intangibles, such as the emotional and economic value of a child to the family as well as other rewards and benefits. A more limited, short-term cost-benefit ratio would be based on computing the savings in government expenditures in year two that might be attributed to the cost of providing family-planning services in year one. Cutright and Jaffe (1977), using 1975 data, pioneered in projecting such figures. Their projections focus on family planning in general; their figures are useful, although they tend to produce underestimates of the ratio. "Benefits" include saved welfare cost of: (1) medical care associated with pregnancy and birth—prenatal care, delivery, postpartum care for the mother, and first-year care of the infant; (2) public assistance for one year for children born to women on public assistance; and (3) selected social services for recipients and their offspring for one year. Costs are the monies necessary to deliver family-planning services for one woman. The criteria produce conservative estimates of the total "benefits" because some women and their infants would be pushed onto welfare as a result of another birth or employment lost during pregnancy, and early child rearing would push still others into eligibility for some public assistance, and so forth.

The minimum estimated government savings, according to Cutright and Jaffe (1976), for 1965 through 1975 equaled nearly $1.1 billion. The cost-benefit ratio becomes more favorable each year, the average being 1:1.8. For 1975, the latest year examined, the ratio was 1:2.5 (i.e., for every $1.00 spent on family-planning in 1975, $2.50 was immediately "saved" in 1976 by the averted births that would have cost taxpayers money for medical care, public assistance, and social services). These were short-term savings; the estimates of long-range savings range from $26 to $100 for every $1 spent.

Without going through the statistical gymnastics to make the analysis relevant for sterilization alone, which is a one-time cost spread over a lifetime of "savings," it is obvious that family-planning programs save the government money. When cost-benefit logic becomes the *raison d'être* of family-planning programs, as critics like Allan Chase (1977) warn, the inexorable logic becomes a population control argument to sterilize more poor women: the more sterilized, the more saved; the younger they are, the more births averted. The 1975 "savings" were 400 million (Cutright and Jaffe 1977); in 1983 dollars that would be about 850 million.

The third part of the impact question concerns demographic consequences. One method would be to contrast birth rates of welfare recipients in 1965 with rates of recent recipients, and then to ascribe the differences to family-planning programs and sterilization as an integral part of those services. Those figures, of all the projections, would be the most untrustworthy because they would isolate one variable and ascribe all the variance to it, thus falling prey to the error of population fetishism. Birth rates for the entire population decreased from 19.4 in 1965 to 14.8 in 1976 and then rose again to 16.2 in 1980. In this period of declining fertility and delayed childbirth for all women, rates declined more rapidly among poor and nearly poor women than among those with incomes above near-poverty level (Jaffe 1974). There is no way to determine precisely how much of this decline can be attributed to the impact of organized programs or sterilization and how much to other factors.

It is possible, however, to estimate the extent to which sterilization limits fertility. To estimate the number of births averted by sterilization, one must make assumptions about the level of fertility that would have prevailed in the absence of sterilization. The question, then, is how many births would theoretically have occurred to sterilized women had they not been sterilized (Westoff and McCarthy 1979). The procedure, suggested by Presser (1969) in her study on Puerto Rico, is to compare the mean number of births of sterilized and unsterilized welfare recipients. For reasons previously given, the most relevant comparisons will be for those with three or more children. The appropriate measure is to compare the fertility of sterilized welfare recipients at different age groups against the fertility of unsterilized women at the end of their reproductive span; the comparisons then refer to completed fertility. Unsterilized women at the

TABLE 5-4

Mean Number of Births for Welfare Mothers with at Least Three Children, at Completed Fertility: 1976

Age in 1976	Sterilized	Unsterilized	Difference at Completed Fertility
15–24	3.14 (a)	3.25	2.87 (e − a)
25–34	4.02 (b)	3.85	1.99 (e − b)
35–44	5.86 (c)	6.01 (e)	.15 (e − c)
Mean	4.84 (d)	4.55	1.17 (e − d)

Source: Original data.

end of their reproductive cycle have a mean number of 6.01 births while the mean of those sterilized in the 24-or-under age group is 3.14, the mean for the 25–34 age group is 4.02, and the mean for the 35–44 age group is 5.86. The completed fertility of sterilized welfare recipients ranges from 2.87 to .15 *fewer* births than for those recipients who are still fertile. These figures are drawn from Table 5-4.

Better dissemination of birth-control information, advances in technology, and the availability of public clinics support the argument that the 35–44 age group experienced higher fertility than similar young women will have experienced by the time they reach that age range; therefore, further modifications are in order. Matching the mean fertility of sterilized welfare recipients of all ages with the fertility of unsterilized recipients at the end of their reproductive span should minimize this gap. Whereas sterilized women of all ages have a mean number of 4.84 births, the mean of those unsterilized in the 35–44 range is 6.01. The completed fertility of sterilized welfare mothers is then roughly 1.17 fewer births per mother. The final calculation is made with the domain assumption that had women not been sterilized they would have experienced fertility rates similar to fertile women. One can only conjecture as to what method sterilized women on welfare would have chosen had they not been sterilized.

There is a difference of about 1.17 births per mother on welfare in completed fertility, which is a conservative estimate. If these differences seem less than spectacular at first glance, one must remember that sterilization was not fully authorized until 1971 and the analyzed data are from 1976. Five years is a short time span for the emergence of impressive long-term demographic consequences. Another study using different procedures and data estimated that sterilization averted roughly 800,000 unwanted births in the United States population from 1971 to 1973 (Westoff and McCarthy 1979). One could conjecture, given the clear pattern and levels of funding, that the fertility difference might widen in years to come. Yet Westoff and Ryder (1977, 162) caution that "increasing sterilization cannot have as marked a demographic impact in a society with modern fertility control as it might under a less effective contraceptive regime," as in Puerto Rico. But if the poor are perceived as being less likely than others to avail themselves of existing opportunities and technology, then the comparative impact is greatest for them.

Prudent judgments are needed before drawing conclusions based on estimates, cost-benefit ratios, and the like. By following constraints and abiding by conservative estimating procedures one can assemble the following case. Welfare-related differentials widen, making the poor more likely to be sterilized than anyone else at any time in American history. Inception of federal programs and policies is instrumental in producing this outcome. There are substantial benefits from "saved" welfare costs from births averted by family planning. The exact ratios and dollars saved can be disputed, not that there is a positive, short-term cost-benefit ratio. The overall demographic impact can be described as slight, thus far. Nonetheless, despite all caution, there is reason to believe that sterilization has lowered birth rates by about 1.17 per welfare recipient.

Cost-benefit analyses and projections are not merely the tools of bureaucrats and academics. "How great an impact the federal programs had is impossible to estimate," Caspar Weinberger, the Secretary of HEW, said in 1974, "but to say a program so widely accepted as that of family planning has had no impact on fertility is plainly unrealistic." He described the program as "remarkably successful," and pointed out that it was cost-effective as well, saving more than two dollars for every dollar spent (*Family Planning Digest* 1974b, 2). His statement is another link in the chain that ties the pattern of services delivered by these programs to social policy objectives. It should be noted that just as sterilization is shown to be cost effective, abortion could also be justified on the same narrow cost-efficiency grounds. But this does not happen, which only indicates the importance of ideological concerns over bureaucratic rationality.

Personal Meanings

Personal meanings should be considered along with broad societal consequences. In 1980 about 4.4 million women received reproductive health care to which they otherwise might not have had access. The quality of reproductive health care delivered by this system was largely unattainable for the poor prior to the 1970s. Such access to reproductive, maternal, and infant health care is unparalleled in American history for this group of women. Obviously, over the years millions of women have benefited from these services. Unwanted pregnancies have been averted, reproductive health care is more thorough, and women and their babies are healthier. The achievement is evident, in spite of limiting factors such as less than ideal quality of services and discriminatory delivery.

The emotional and physical stress of childbirth or abortion makes women more vulnerable to a sterilization they will later regret. An early study (cited in Sigelman 1981), revealed that 14 percent of women who consented to a sterilization during caesarian section unequivocally regretted the operation. Several experts have concluded that the psychological prospects are better "when a decision for a sterilization is not made under the pressure of time and circumstance such as labor or childbirth" (Sigelman 1981, 17).

Similarly, Schwyhart and Kutner (1973), after reviewing twenty-two studies from different countries, found that the highest incidence of regret was expressed by women who had been sterilized concomitantly with an abortion. McCoy (1968, 1054) quotes a British woman who was sterilized at the time of abortion and later regretted her decision: "My feelings on sterilization are impossible to express. No man can possibly know what it is like to be left a mere shell of a woman." Furthermore, there is statistical evidence of higher mortality and morbidity when abortion is combined with sterilization (Savage 1982, 295). Barnes and Zuspan found that when sterilization was proposed by the attending physician, 32 percent of sterilized patients were unhappy, compared to 9 percent if the idea originated with the woman or her mate (Barnes and Zuspan 1958).

Countless studies have confirmed that age is correlated with rates of regret. In one study, 25 percent of patients under twenty-six were subsequently dissatisfied with their sterilization, compared to only 5 percent of an older group. In another study, over 50 percent of women requesting reversals were twenty-five or under (Sigelman 1981).

Regret is especially high among young women with few children. Gomel (1978) found that a change in marital status was the reason 63 percent of the women he studied wanted to be fertile again. New relationships or new marriages were the most prevalent reasons women wanted to regain the ability to bear children. The factor of youth increases severalfold the chances of divorce or remarriage—events likely to have a significant impact on future decisions to have additional children.

A recent major study by Carlson and Vickers (1982) found widespread misconceptions about the irreversibility of sterilization, especially among blacks, Hispanics, and lower-class women. They found a shocking lack of information about the permanence of sterilization. Overall, 38.5 percent did not know sterilization is permanent. Among black women the figure was 45 percent; Hispanics, 59 percent; whites, 24 percent. Thirty-eight percent said they would not make the same decision today on the basis of what they have learned since the operation. The regret rate for minority women was even higher: 40 percent for black women and 51.7 percent for Hispanic women. This rate was found to be related to age, information, and the amount of time between reaching the decision and having the operation. Among sterilized women in general, those sterilized within three days after reaching a decision showed a regret rate of 56 percent compared with 26 percent for those who waited more than a month (Carlson and Vickers 1982).

Estimates of regret fluctuate wildly according to different definitions of what constitutes "regret" and the sample studied. The range varies from over 50 percent among Hispanic women in New York City and young women generally to claims of virtually no dissatisfaction (Rodriquez-Trias 1978; Population Reports 1980).

To the assessment of societal consequences must be added a notion of personal meaning. Here again, the results carry a dual message. While millions have benefited from the expansion of reproductive health care services, there is a substantial regret factor among those sterilized.

6
The Movement against Abuse

IN LATE SEPTEMBER of 1977 over one hundred individuals representing fifty organizations met in Washington, D.C., to address the issue of sterilization abuse. Delegates came from all parts of the country to the National Conference on Sterilization Abuse, which was organized by the Interreligious Foundation for Community Organization. Those attending represented women's organizations, church social action groups, the feminist health movement, minority women, native Americans, alternative media, family-planning organizations, and reproductive-rights groups (see Appendix). Ultimately, the conference was instrumental in strengthening federal actions to guard against sterilization abuse.

In one version of events, Joseph Califano, then secretary of Health, Education, and Welfare (HEW), took sole credit for the federal action. In his memoirs, *Governing America*, Califano claims that "to stem the widespread resort to sterilization by many doctors, particularly on poor women, I issued regulations sharply restricting funding of that procedure. All agreed that informed consent by the patient is a necessary ingredient in any decision about sterilization" (Califano 1981, 208). This reform, like most, should be viewed as a response to a popular social movement organized to redress social injustice.

Because of mounting pressure related to the Relf case and publicity of the 1972 guideline snafu, HEW decided in 1974 to release regulations on sterilization procedures. These rules prohibited sterilization of people under twenty-one or who, for whatever reason, could not legally consent. They stipulated a seventy-two-hour waiting period between the granting of consent and the procedure. Informed consent, including a statement that guarded against threatened revocation of welfare if not sterilized, had to be obtained in writing. These precautions applied to federally financed sterilizations only.

As has been shown previously, several studies demonstrated that these perfunctory regulations were unmonitored and unenforced, and that a vast majority of hospitals were not in compliance. The problem had become a public issue, but there were no grounds to expect that abusive practices would change.

A large number of sterilizations were being performed in New York City hospitals, particularly those serving black and Puerto Rican communities. This prompted Esta Armstrong, of the office of quality assurance at the Health and Hospital Corporation (HHC), the New York City agency responsible for municipal hospitals, to convene a meeting of interested parties. In late 1974 and early 1975, the Ad Hoc Advisory Committee on Sterilization Guidelines was formed. The group's members were from the American Civil Liberties Union, the Center for Constitutional Rights, the Committee to End Sterilization Abuse (CESA), Healthright, HealthPac, and the community boards of the hospitals and also included other interested professionals. Most were women involved in patient advocacy or health-care reform, and they represented a cross section of New York's various ethnic communities.

The ad hoc group first investigated sterilization practices within the twenty municipal hospitals overseen by HHC. "We began pulling out stuff [information about abuse] and it was like striking oil because each hospital used its own surgical consent form," recalls Esta Armstrong. Furthermore, there was "no way of measuring the impact of federal regulations because the feds were not looking at them, much less the hospitals themselves" (Armstrong interview

1983). The group then analyzed the process by which abuse takes place and compiled this information in a report, "Why Sterilization Guidelines are Needed" (Ad Hoc Advisory Committee on Sterilization Guidelines 1975).

The ad hoc committee located the flaws in existing HEW regulations. They found that consents generally were obtained around the time of abortion or childbirth, periods of stress during which women could not leave the "captive" hospital environment to discuss options with friends, family, neighbors, or outside health experts. They reasoned that medical advice could be coercive if given only in a hospital setting because the vocabulary and amount of information given could be controlled and confusing. Given these findings, the ad hoc coalition decided to draft and advocate more stringent regulations for municipal hospitals in New York. Esta Armstrong reasoned that "when you are working within a hospital setting, you work on procedural stuff. Hospitals respond to protocol" (Armstrong interview 1983).

The drafted guidelines called for a thirty-day waiting period; prohibited consent concurrent with child delivery, abortion, or hospitalization for a major procedure; stipulated full counseling on all birth-control options; and required informational materials to be in the language preferred by the woman. If she desired, the woman could bring a patient advocate as well as a person of her own choosing to witness the consent procedure. She was asked on the consent form to express her understanding of the procedure, especially its permanence.

While no one from the coalition really thought such regulations could be implemented, they were unprepared for the ferocity of the opposition, the strongest of which came from obstetricians, hospital administrators, and organizations active in family planning and population control. Planned Parenthood, the Association for Voluntary Sterilization (AVS), and others responded with angry letters and telegrams (Rodriguez-Trias 1978). Opposition came, surprisingly, from feminists and women's organizations, such as some chapters of the National Organization for Women (N.O.W.) and the National Abortion Rights Action League (NARAL). "The feminist groups were ready to kill us," Armstrong says, because they felt guidelines were patronizing, that women did not need a thirty-day wait to make up their minds. The American College of Obstetricians and Gynecologists (ACOG), Ob-Gyn departmental chiefs, and hospital administrators also had a strong negative reaction to the proposed reforms. Lawsuits were threatened, and one was filed. There was "very heavy reaction to guidelines that were not yet passed—they weren't even passed" (Armstrong interview 1983).

The thirty-day waiting period is the most divisive issue feminists have had to face on the abuse issue. Some argue that a thirty-day waiting period is paternalistic (women do not need that long to make up their minds) and that it interferes with delivery of the service on demand. Others consider the thirty-day wait unnecessary as a safeguard when weighed against the added expense and increased medical risk that may result from "double surgery" (i.e., the sterilization could have been performed during an operation).

In the face of opposition from a number of sources, a fragile but determined coalition formed to enact the proposed regulations. At this point, "fortunately for us," in Armstrong's assessment, "CESA came into being." Passage of the HHC regulations was dependent upon popular reaction. The Committee to End Sterilization Abuse helped to mobilize popular support among New York City's public hospital clientele. "Community boards (representing NYC municipal hospitals) were decisive," Armstrong feels, because "these were the recipients of the care." These were people whose voices were heard by the HHC board. When a Belleview hospital community board says "we represent Belleview hospital and we want to see guidelines passed," it makes a tremendous impression. This pressure counteracted the medical groups because the clients knew the issue. Abuse became defined as a social issue, not simply a medical one. The regulations were passed by the HHC board and became effective in November of 1975.

As consciousness of sterilization abuse grew, the movement supported further legislation, the first expression of which was in New York City. Legislation was drawn up, extending the stricter regulations to all New York City private and public health facilities. A change either in HHC administrations or in mayors could render existing hospital regulations null and void, but legislation would make them the law. New York City Councilman Carter Burden introduced the bill, whose passage was supported by social forces similar to those that had supported the HHC regulation. The opposition, for the most part, was familiar; however, the issue of sterilization abuse and regulations was becoming more visible, public, and highly politicized. The social movement against sterilization abuse was led by CESA with the support of the women's health movement, especially the newly organized network of feminist health centers, and some women's rights activists. The primary opposition, again, came from the established organizations of the medical profession, family-planning associations and providers, and population-control groups.

Public hearings on the Burden Bill were held in fall 1976 and spring 1977. The proposed law called for extending HHC guidelines to all New York City health facilities. Three sets of hearings were broadcast over public radio and received substantial coverage in other media; CESA, in charge of organizing support for the measure, stacked the hearing rooms with supporters and lined up people to submit testimony. Experts as well as abused welfare recipients presented their views. The hearings had a theatrical flare because, as one CESA activist noted, it was "important to put on a good show— this is how you get legislation passed."

The show of public hearings was made possible by diligent preparation to construct awareness of abuse, to persuade people of the issue's importance, and to convince some organizations to take a strong position. The most significant example of this persuasion occurred in the New York City branch of N.O.W., which had not endorsed previous HHC regulations, where CESA made a presentation on the issue. The N.O.W. health committee in New York, convinced that the potential for abuse was far more serious than the inconvenience of having to wait for the procedure, endorsed the Burden Bill. At the hearings Councilman Burden read a letter from N.O.W.- New York that strongly endorsed the bill by distinguishing between sterilization and abortion. Broad and diverse support also came from groups such as the American Civil Liberties Union

(ACLU), Physicians Forum, Women United for Action, and National Black Feminists.

The opposition was narrower, often limited to specific interests, and not as well organized. The Association for Voluntary Sterilization sent its associate director to say that AVS had not yet decided on a position and to ask city council for a delay. Burden noted that "the principal and certainly most effective lobbyist against this bill has been Planned Parenthood." Their integrity on this matter was suspect since Planned Parenthood had applied to perform sterilizations in its outpatient clinics. But the application to perform sterilizations, according to Burden, "was rejected . . . because Planned Parenthood refused to adhere to certain criteria set down by the committee—including a thirty-day waiting period" (cited in Rodriguez-Trias 1978, 15). The bill was passed thirty-eight to zero with three abstentions.

During the National Conference on Sterilization Abuse, September 1977, in Washington, D.C., representatives from the conference met with officials from HEW. Veterans of the HHC and New York City campaigns told HEW what kind of regulations were needed. After regional hearings were held in 1978, HEW issued regulations for all federally funded sterilizations (45 C.F.R. Section 1392; 42 C.F.R. Sections 50, 441). Informed consent about the procedure and alternatives was to be provided in the preferred language of the client; consent could not be obtained during labor; a thirty-day waiting period was mandated; and there was a moratorium on sterilizing people under the age of twenty-one.

A movement modeled from local concerns in New York City municipal hospitals developed ultimately into national regulations for federally financed procedures. Impetus for this movement was provided by national publicity and concern over early cases of flagrant abuse; health care advocates, some women's rights groups, and a women's health movement pressed the issue as one among many that concerned them. A coalition of groups forced the issue. In the forefront of this movement that won regulations to prevent abuse was CESA, the committee that shaped the issue, defined the debate, and provided mobilization. The social movement's success thus warrants analysis of CESA's role.

The following examination of CESA, which proceeds along several vantage points, relies mostly on the recollections of key participants—not because their version is necessarily more pristine, but because it is important to know what people believed to have happened and how their perceptions shaped actions and events. This information was verified and augmented with that of existing literature and CESA's own documents.[1] Because other voices were heard and other forms of political activity were evident, the dynamic anti-abuse movement should not be equated with CESA, which, nonetheless, was its mainspring. This movement gained one of the most concrete, if limited, successes of radical and feminist groups in the 1970s.

CESA

The Committee to End Sterilization Abuse was formed during 1974 and 1975 in New York. The leadership and inner core of CESA was composed mainly of women who came from different social movements to work on the sterilization issue. They came from various legal and health care reform groups, such as the Center for Constitutional Rights and the Medical Committee for Human Rights; political movements, such as the Puerto Rican Socialist party; and organizations concerned with women's issues. Helen Rodriguez-Trias, Karen Stamm, and Nancy Stearns were among the most visible and articulate leaders. While the HHC regulations presupposed that abuses resulted almost entirely from reckless medical practice, and hence could be remedied by forcing the medical system to be more responsible, CESA placed abuse within a larger and more critical political and social context. The doctor-patient relationship was seen as only one source of the problem. The issue was broadened to encompass population control, doctors as instruments of social control, and sterilization as a response to cuts in social benefits and services.

Initially, in New York, another of the central impulses was a predominant "anti-imperialist" perspective that focused on Puerto Rican independence, an emphasis that shifted by early 1976. One signal incident changed the focus: CESA was invited to a church in Harlem to speak about sterilization abuse. Faced with an all black audience, CESA realized that it was absurd to focus exclusively on Puerto Rico because abuse was an issue for poor and minority women in the United States. Concurrently, members of the Puerto Rican Socialist party withdrew from CESA to concentrate their energies elsewhere. Assisting the Puerto Rican independence movement remained important, although it became subsidiary.

In a statement of purpose, CESA clearly defined itself as both radical and feminist. "In a variety of ways the U.S. ruling class denies us our rights to choose the best available method of birth control. One of these ways is by sterilization abuse." Helen Rodriguez-Trias, one of CESA's architects, says: "CESA groped toward a class analysis." Sterilization abuse "was not seen as a human rights issue," because it was more important to see whom "it was happening to and why, and to examine what this meant in terms of maintaining society as it is" (Rodriguez-Trias interview 1983). Abuse, then, is broadly interpreted to mean the biasing of services along class, racial, and ethnic lines—the limiting of freedom of choice for the poor.

> Forced infertility is in no way a substitute for a good job, enough to
> eat, decent education, daycare, medical services, maternal infant
> care, housing, clothing, or cultural integrity. We support the right of
> the individual to choose the method of birth control she or he prefers.
> But when the society does not provide the basic necessities of life for
> everyone, there can be no such freedom of choice [CESA Papers].

The committee saw an irreconcilable conflict between population control, of which sterilization abuse was the latest manifestation, and the right of women to control their own reproductive capacity. Through population-control programs a major aspect of female gender identity is taken from women. A sharp distinction was made between CESA's opposition to programs of discriminatory population control and its support for all forms of birth control.

The increased funding of sterilizations and the decision not to fund abortion in 1978 is seen as evidence of a de facto policy of population control that most directly affects the poor and minorities. The rise in sterilizations and the defunding of abortions must be viewed as two sides of the same coin. The question is put very bluntly: "In the absence of abortion, adequate birth control, decent childcare, health care, and adequate incomes, can we assume that the rise in sterilization amongst most women affected is a result of 'free choice'?" (Committee for Abortion Rights and Against Sterilization Abuse 1979, 52). CESA's objectives reflected its deep-rooted analysis of the reasons for abuse, and a primary goal was the immediate elimination of overt, flagrant abuses. It was also important to stir other people and groups into action, especially women's and health care groups. Services were provided for those that inquired, such as lawyers for the abused and counselors for those who sought advice.

Other goals were less concrete. It was important to educate or "raise consciousness" about population-control ideology, which was seen as one response to environmental and social problems. Population control was seen as racist, degrading to women's health, obfuscating class issues, and subverting movements for social change. On reproductive issues CESA wanted to separate population-control groups from the women's movement. One unstated goal was to unify the radical feminist movement and Third World communities on an issue of common interest. To do so, some thought it necessary to remove the influence that groups like the Planned Parenthood Federation of America traditionally had on the women's movement.

Planned Parenthood sees itself as a progressive, liberal organization besieged by both the Right and the feminist movement. Planned Parenthood has always been viewed with suspicion within the feminist and women's health movements, by groups like CESA, because of its involvement in and association with population control, both at home and abroad. Furthermore, as Sheryl Ruzek (1978a) notes, it has played a major role in testing, dispensing, and promoting the widespread use of hazardous contraceptives, highlighting that the social conditions of birth control are not determined by women them-

selves but by professionals and pharmaceutical companies. Planned
Parenthood represents a narrow professional and medical approach
to fertility control, one that directly conflicts with a woman-centered,
self-help diffusion of knowledge. Angela Davis recalls Planned Parenthood's legacy of subordinating minority rights to the interests of
individual white, middle-class women (Davis 1981). Planned Parenthood affiliates in many parts of the country stridently opposed
sterilization regulations; nevertheless, ambivalence is directed toward the organization because local affiliates are somewhat independent, their sensitivity to women's and minority-rights issues not
always reflecting that of the national organization. Planned Parenthood is an important and trusted ally on the issue of abortion
rights; in periods of prohibition or legal restriction (pre-1973 and
post-Hyde Amendment, 1977), there is a tendency to unite on the
basis of keeping abortion legal, safe, and accessible. Even during
periods of cooperation, many CESA members felt that old and established allies might hinder development of more radical directions for
the women's movement.

After many internal discussions and debates CESA decided upon
regulations as a concrete focus, a decision that was periodically re-
examined. Karen Stamm, a leading activist, explains the thinking behind this focus: "We had the vehicle of regulations. Had we confined
our discussion to an ideological one, many people might not have
taken us seriously" (Stamm interview 1983). CESA reasoned that
the most appropriate structure for simultaneously tackling the concrete issue of abuse and broader ideological issues would be a core-
based, collective organization.

After CESA decided to pursue the regulation strategy, the organization was fully committed to winning new regulations. Activities
ranged from gathering signatures on petitions and writing letters to
organizing public meetings and demonstrations, efforts that began to
elicit support from other organizations. In an internal assessment of
the New York City guideline campaign, CESA enumerated major
obstacles, which included a general confusion of birth control with
population control, the influence of population-control ideas within
the women's movement, the prestige of Planned Parenthood, the

general saturation of population-control ideas in the mass media, and its own lack of access to major media (CESA Papers).

Many women's, civil liberty, and Third World groups endorsed the Burden Bill. A key turning point was the endorsement by N.O.W. in New York. Other important factors included politics both in New York City and the health services, as well as the role played by Councilman Burden. Right-to-Life groups lent quiet, unsolicited support. One councilman remarked that since both the N.O.W.–New York and Right-to-Life groups supported the bill, he couldn't possibly miss the opportunity to simultaneously please such diverse constituencies. Such an opportunity was rare, indeed.

Aside from the protection it afforded women, passage of the New York City regulations resulted in gains for CESA and the entire anti-abuse movement. Internally, CESA grew as an organization. The core group in New York doubled to twenty and inner cohesion solidified; members learned how to maneuver in the legislative arena and how to wield power. CESA built a strong network of support that had been available but could only be tapped on the basis of concrete work. The organization assumed leadership on the sterilization issue, which produced widespread recognition, respect, and legitimacy for themselves and the issue. In the process, CESA was transformed from an educational to an action organization.

CESA learned from the passage of the Burden Bill that national regulations would be preferable to a community-by-community approach. In addition, members believed they could pressure HEW to adopt similar regulations by arguing that such a law was working in New York City.

The national prominence attained by CESA, which was not a national organization, was ironic. A loose confederation of independent groups—some calling themselves CESA, others using similar names—worked on the sterilization issue between 1974 and 1978. They were located in Boston, New Haven, Hartford, Philadelphia, western Massachusetts, Baltimore, Chicago, Saint Louis, and elsewhere. Groups on the West Coast tended to use names other than CESA, such as Sterilization and Informed Consent Rights. All these groups were autonomous, and they worked on issues of local concern. For instance, the CESA group in western Massachusetts focused on the sterilization of Hispanics while the group in Saint Louis concentrated on an Agency for International Development (A.I.D.)–funded international training program in sterilization techniques at Washington University. All groups coalesced to lobby, testify, and agitate for nationwide HEW regulations in 1978.

Groups in New York and elsewhere disbanded between 1978 and 1980 for two reasons: (1) with the promulgation of HEW regulations in 1978, the battle over abuse, when defined as flagrant, coercive, or nonconsensual, appeared to be won; and (2) Medicaid abortions were banned in 1978. The renewed urgency of the abortion issue redirected the emphasis of many reproductive-rights activists and women's organizations. In some cases, as in New York, the demise of CESA was hastened by internal problems. While CESA no longer exists, many former activists continue their efforts within other organizations and on other forums. The Committee for Abortion Reform and Against Sterilization Abuse (CARASA) was started around the time of the debate on the Hyde Amendment to cut Medicaid funds for abortion. By the time CARASA became organized, the movement against abuse was already on the verge of winning reform regulations. The work of CARASA has been important in linking the contradiction of abortion restrictions and sterilization availability to a feminist understanding of reproductive rights. CARASA coexisted with and then superseded CESA; many former CESA activists became involved in CARASA.

Achievements of the Movement Against Abuse

Former CESA activists point to significant achievements in the movement against abuse, foremost of which are the regulations—HHC, New York City, and HEW—to stop flagrant, coercive abuses. While it is hard to measure the precise impact of these regulations, the reduced number of lawsuits and the lack of publicity about overt cases like the Relfs is an indication of their success. Regulations, however, were never meant to address the patterning of class and race differences, nor were they intended to change basic economic and social conditions. Having regulations on the books and enforcing them are separate matters; the movement against abuse could get regulations passed but could not insure that they would be enforced.

A second area of achievement involves the quantity and quality of services CESA was able to offer. Members acted as counselors and patients'-rights and legal advocates, and they offered referrals. Community organizations and church groups flooded CESA with requests for speakers; in one year alone, they spoke at over one hundred public functions. After these speeches people from the audience often talked about how they had been abused.

Victory in a contest for power forced concessions from population controllers and the organized medical profession, causing them to lose credibility on this issue. The influence of population-control organizations on some quarters of the women's movement was diminished because they were seen as being on the wrong side of issues involving social justice and racial equality. As a result, their legitimacy as part of the women's movement was questioned. Members of CESA felt they succeeded in making population-control groups tone down their propaganda. Many believed, for example, that AVS reduced efforts to retain public legitimacy because it recognized the validity of concerns about abuse. Forcing AVS to admit that abuse was a problem for poor women was a major victory, which dampened the knee-jerk Malthusian impulse to solve population-related problems by curtailing the fertility of the poor. In the battle for guidelines, at least in New York City and a few other cities, populationists were separated from the women's movement.

The anti-abuse movement made major inroads in debunking population-control ideas, and this is most evident in women's and health-care organizations. The issue has been integrated into the concerns of reproductive rights and health care reform groups, and they are generally critical of population control.

CESA educated other organizations about the uses of sterilization and galvanized them into action, thus tranforming a private problem into a public issue. The political struggles over sterilization abuse led by feminist, black, and Third World groups have had an impact on women's consciousness.

Events in Puerto Rico during the lifetime of CESA have kept the issue of independence on a "back burner." One enduring result of CESA's work, however, is that the independence movement has become more aware of how population control contributes to oppression in Puerto Rico. This awareness gives women's issues more weight in the independence movement because population control is seen as an instrument of national and class oppression (Mass 1976; Rodriguez-Trias interview 1983).

The goal of building contact and unity between the women's movement and Third World communities proved to be ephemeral. CESA bridged these groups because sterilization abuse was perceived as being rampant in minority communities, but the connection has been lost. Karen Stamm notes that the focus on abortion as a single issue since 1978 draws a different social base of support and interest. Abortion, if seen only as an individual rights issue, may be less compatible with the concerns of minority groups. Thus, historical dilemmas within the women's movement have resurfaced. There is a different approach in attempting to protect rights for individuals versus securing rights for a group or class of people. Activists in reproductive politics confront a philosophical tension between individual choice and preventing the abuse of groups. One activist says that protection from abuse involves the "socialization of responsibility" (Petchesky 1984, 191). Stamm feels there are class, racial, and ethnic differences between abortion-rights and sterilization-abuse constituencies. Population-control advocates have again become an ally on the abortion issue.

By confronting the abuse problem within the contexts of reproductive health care, women's rights, and population control, CESA and its allies were asking the whole women's movement to closely examine its friends and foes. In CARASA's words,

> The political history surrounding the establishment of the federal
> and New York City guidelines reveals that, where sterilization is con-
> cerned there are fundamental differences of principle between the
> groups who have supported liberalized abortion. In general, groups
> promoting population control (e.g., Planned Parenthood, NARAL,

and the AVS) do not support the regulation [Committee for Abortion Rights and Against Sterilization Abuse 1979, 54].

CESA, CARASA, and others became highly critical of groups, such as Planned Parenthood, NARAL, and AVS, that had been the traditional supporters of the women's movement on the abortion issue, but who were now opposed to regulations protecting women against sterilization abuse. This turned into a two-way street when Right-to-Lifers supported stringent sterilization regulations. This support, though unsolicited, was nonetheless a source of trouble for CESA, which was accused of being a closet Right-to-Life group.

Feminist reaction to forced sterilization developed slowly because it did not directly threaten white middle-class feminists. In addition, the population-control organizations that promoted sterilization were needed allies in abortion repeal (Ruzek 1978b). One of CESA's most important contributions was to sensitize segments of the women's movement to the class and racial concerns surrounding abuse. Esta Armstrong's incisive observation about the bulk of the women's movement illustrates this concern:

> Their reasoning was at the time confused between the struggle on abortion rights and the abuse around sterilization. Many of them were too far removed from the minority community to recognize the significance of sterilization abuse. They were not prepared to recognize, in fact, that there was a bigger issue Third World women were facing, other than abortion [Armstrong interview 1983].

Helen Rodriguez-Trias concurs, adding that the abuse issue "forced them to confront their racist biases and class attitudes. There is no doubt of it, that one of CESA's major contributions was in shaping up the women's movement" (Rodriguez-Trias interview 1983).

Sheryl Ruzek argues that the most fundamental value conflict within feminism at large stems from the movement's race and class composition. "Although many feminists choose to believe that sisterhood will unite women of all backgrounds, the reality is that sisterhood may be powerful," she notes, "but so are race, class, and status in shaping perceptions of what constitute problems as well as possible solutions" (Ruzek 1978b, 183). Sterilization abuse is an issue that confronts the complex relationship between race, class, and gender. The women's movement had to face the issue in its full complexity, and neither CESA nor the anti-abuse movement can claim full credit for this because many groups were developing an awareness of class and race issues as a part of their internal political processes. Helen Rodriguez-Trias observes, however, that "the sterilization issue was more important than practically any other issue in waking people up to the uses of racism and to an understanding of hierarchy. . . . They understood power relationships better" (Rodriguez-Trias interview 1983).

As part of the struggle to make abortion legal and safe, prior to 1973, an ideological and tactical consensus had emerged. Petchesky notes that the population-control movement was pushing on one side and feminist health-movement activists were pushing on the other. Masses of women were violating the law and obtaining abortions. What emerged was a philosophy that removed the state from abortion decisions altogether, and relied on the laissez faire notion that the "right to choose" will guarantee good, safe abortions (Petchesky 1984). This framework saw women battling to attain a right to a service that was denied them by a sexist state; therefore, any barrier to the service was oppressive to all women. In this perspective all women had a common interest in abortion and could unite around it. Once indelibly a fixture of the women's movement, this framework, in CESA's opinion, was translated into resisting any safeguards to sterilization. The political solution to the unavailability of abortion became reified as a philosophy and was transplanted onto an issue with an entirely different social context and history, thus some women's groups wanted no restrictions on the delivery of sterilization (i.e., no regulations, no waiting period, etc.). Explaining the historical and contextual differences between abortion and sterilization assumed vital importance. Ultimately, regulations serve to alter access to, and control over, services. According to Ruzek, the question is not whether or not specific laws or regulations are in the best interests of women, but, rather, in which women's interests and under what specific circumstances.

Although it was easy to attack the women's movement for its lack of class and racial sensitivities, CESA recognized its importance. Even with the gamut of politics it represented, the women's movement always provided a forum on which sterilization could be debated (Rodriguez-Trias interview 1983). The New York City chapter of N.O.W. dramatically took a strong position on the issue, thus symbolizing CESA's success in making a significant distinction between abortion and sterilization. When AVS informed the New York City hearing that N.O.W. in California was opposed to its state regulations some council members expressed concern. Realizing the pivotal importance of N.O.W. on this issue, CESA assembled a high-powered delegation of feminist doctors, lawyers, and healthcare activists to make a formal presentation to N.O.W. in New York. Denise Fuge, then head of the health committee and later president of N.O.W. in New York, was very sympathetic and sensitive to the issue of abuse. Knowledgeable about medical inequality because of her work in a large medical complex, Fuge was instrumental in persuading N.O.W.-New York to take a position. At the last hearing, during a lull in the testimony, Burden read N.O.W.'s letter of support into the record. "While we are wary of government interference in matters relating to fertility," the letter stated, "certainly a distinction must be made between laws designed to insure freedom of choice and access to family-planning information and methods and laws which restrict choice or limit access. This bill seeks to increase freedom, not limit it" (N.O.W.-New York, 1977). One observer fondly remembers watching AVS and Planned Parenthood representatives "writhe" in their seats while the letter was being read, moaning "Oh God, those stupid women in N.O.W."

The opposition of AVS was expected, but that of Planned Parenthood was more troubling, especially in light of its consistent support of abortion rights. At the time of the Burden legislation AVS and Planned Parenthood had established a loan fund, each pledging $300,000 in conjunction with a local bank in order to convert freestanding outpatient abortion clinics into free-standing outpatient sterilization clinics. It seems that Planned Parenthood's objections to regulations were not entirely philosophical, as a thirty-day waiting

period might seriously jeopardize the financial operations of outpatient clinics.

New York State Assemblyman Mark Siegel, in 1977, introduced
a sterilization bill purporting to safeguard against potential abuses.
His bill formally called for a thirty-day wait, but with a seventy-two
hour exception for any procedures that "unexpectedly take place before the thirty-day period has elapsed." Many groups were outraged
at what they saw as an attempt to circumvent the New York City law
and the proposed HEW regulations by creating a legal loophole to
the thirty-day wait. Joan Kelley of the Ad Hoc Women's Studies
Committee Against Sterilization Abuse pointed out that Siegel served
on and had consulted with the board of AVS on the legislation. She
wrote a public letter to Assemblyman Siegel saying that the people of
New York "should know that AVS and Planned Parenthood have set
up a $700,000 loan fund for the establishment of out-of-hospital ster-
ilization clinics. It is evident to us that your bill, which reduces the
age limit to eighteen years and the waiting period to seventy-two
hours, is designed for these clinics" (CESA Papers). CARASA and
CESA wrote to Siegel, also pointing out his AVS board membership
and the AVS–Planned Parenthood plan to open clinics, charging that
his "bill is designed to allow such clinics to operate with a minimum
of regulations" (CESA Papers). His bill was defeated.

The thirty-day wait, an issue that has divided N.O.W., was first
brought to its national meeting in the summer of 1978 because the
organization had not testified on behalf of proposed HEW regulations; many N.O.W. activists wanted the organization to take a
strong position against abuse. Denise Fuge, president of N.O.W. in
New York in 1981 and 1982, saw abuse both as an attack on women
and as a civil rights issue. She argued before N.O.W. that the "entire
women's health movement was behind this issue and that N.O.W.
would look terrible if it did not support the thirty days." She "couldn't
believe the insensitivity and lack of understanding" from N.O.W.'s
leadership on this issue, and fought for a resolution that would put
N.O.W. on record as supporting the reform package, including the
thirty-day period. The resolution lost by 38 out of 546 votes. Fuge
remembers that the debate was very heated and that the opposition

harassed and tried to physically intimidate her (Fuge interview 1983).

Segments of N.O.W. adamantly oppose the thirty-day stipulation because they feel it is paternalistic; other issues, such as the Equal Rights Amendment and abortion rights, have taken precedence over sterilization abuse. Denise Fuge sees N.O.W.'s dilemma as a choice of either "looking good to minority women" or "not going against Planned Parenthood—that is where the pressure comes from" (Fuge interview 1983). She says that N.O.W. opposed activism on sterilization regulations during 1977 and 1978 because some members have close ties with Planned Parenthood. The latter's money and N.O.W.'s ability to mobilize people and volunteers have formed an alliance of mutual needs. According to Fuge, most N.O.W. members would rather keep the organization strong than risk losing an important base of support by pressing the sterilization issue, thereby alienating Planned Parenthood.

Feminist staff attorneys of the Center for Constitutional Rights, disturbed by N.O.W.'s failure to support safeguards in 1978, reminded the organization that they had been at the forefront of the battle to "eliminate barriers to abortion and truly voluntary sterilization as well as to prevent sterilization abuse" and are sensitive to the problems concerning fertility control regulations. But, on the other hand, they implored N.O.W., "where there is a demonstrated history of and propensity toward abuse, it would be a devastating and irreparable error to treat regulation of permanent means of fertility control in the same way as temporary measures" (CESA Papers). In 1984, N.O.W. was still struggling with this issue. Fuge, a member of N.O.W.'s national board, is structuring a method to educate membership so that they may take a stand on the issue.

The attack on and defunding of abortion and the renewed campaign to keep it safe, legal, and available for all have apparently healed some of the wounds resulting from the divisiveness over the regulation fight and the thirty-day stipulation. This renewed struggle has brought some feminist groups and liberal birth-control organizations closer together. In a letter to the executive vice president of Planned Parenthood in New York, CARASA reminded him that "we have publicly agreed to refrain from any lobbying action on state sterilization legislation until after the abortion crisis is resolved" (CESA Papers). CARASA charged Planned Parenthood with violating the agreement; the latter responded that the crisis was temporarily resolved in New York, thus obviating all agreements.

Ruzek's question about regulations being in the interests of some women and not others is incisive—and troubling. The history of the birth-control movement shows that militants, radicals, and activists like Emma Goldman paved the way and paid the price for legalizing birth control. Moderates rode the backs of activists, then crowded them out of the movement and defined birth control through the eyes of conservative, eugenics organizations and supporters. Petchesky's judgment is that feminists "in the campaign for legal abortion won the battle but not the war," because the medical and neo-Malthusian justifications for abortion prevail while the feminist voice is "barely audible" (Petchesky 1984, 131). Some radical feminists say that abortion rights became vulnerable because the women's movement was deradicalized in a process whereby organizations that consolidated the victory of radicals and activists had different agendas (Blair 1977). Was the same pattern being repeated with the movement against abuse? In which women's interests, to paraphrase Ruzek, was it to talk about abortion but to be mute on sterilization abuse? The abortion and sterilization issues are clearly connected. What separates them are the interests of women of different class and color and the organizations that represent those interests. Availability of legal and safe abortions is a problem for all women; federal funding for abortions is a problem more specifically for poor women; and sterilization abuse is a problem almost exclusively for poor women.

The right-to-life view is not just that abuse is wrong but that *all* sterilizations are sinful. They believe that no one voluntarily seeks information about sterilization; therefore, the correct path is to withhold all information, which is exactly opposite CESA's view. Right-to-Lifers want no government involvement in reproductive health care, thus they saw the movement against abuse as an opportunity to appear concerned about social justice. While the surface similarities between CESA and Right-to-Lifers vanish upon close inspection, CESA wanted to insure that it would not be mistaken for part of the Right-to-Life movement or be confused as its ally. For entirely different strategic motivations CESA and Right-to-Lifers shared a common interest in passing safeguards, but they looked like allies, which confused some people. Initially, CESA handled this shared interest poorly by accepting their support; for example, Right-to-Lifers were welcomed at the National Conference on Sterilization Abuse and virtually no one complained when they testified in favor of very restrictive HEW regulations. This was quickly seen as a political blunder that would allow population control groups to equate CESA with the right-to-life position of wanting restrictions on all reproductive health care. In some parts of the country this posed more problems than in others. In Saint Louis, for instance, one local Right-to-Life congressman's offer to support CESA's local campaign was seen as an opportunistic gesture to garner support based upon CESA's hard work. But rejecting any association with him proved futile on the local level, as he was invited to give a speech and bask in the limelight at the National Conference on Sterilization Abuse in Washington, D.C. This inconsistency in the social movement, no doubt a negative consequence of the arrangement of loose confederation, further entangled and confused the abuse issue with the Right-to-Lifers. In New York the experience was different, however, as radical-feminist organizations were stronger and the lines of separation were more distinct.

These gains were not without costs. Population-control organizations began to harass CESA, charging that the committee opposed all sterilizations in the same way that anti-abortion groups object to all abortions. The Brooklyn chapter of N.O.W., which did not endorse the New York City legislation, implied that CESA was a "front" for other unnamed interests. They called CESA "a group which is greatly influenced by extreme left-wing organizations" (CESA Papers). In a similar instance CESA activists were attacked by the leadership of one of the more traditional reproductive-rights groups, NARAL, for being "radicals." One obstetrician asserted that the campaign for regulations was a "Puerto Rican communist plot" (Stamm interview 1983). Many came to CESA with a Marxist perspective and had connections with left-wing groups, but these smear attempts failed to deflect attention from the real issue of abuse. Another form of harassment was the threat of lawsuits by established medical and family-planning organizations to negate the effects of regulations. CESA's preoccupation with regulations resulted in the neglect of other work within the organization; internal matters and long-term projects became secondary, thereby intensifying internal frictions over the allocation of resources (CESA Papers). So many requests for referrals, advice, and speakers poured into the organization during and after the New York City campaign that CESA could not possibly respond to all of them.

Opportunities for Success and Structural Limitations

Why did the movement against abuse succeed in one respect and fail in another? The movement did not occur in a social and political vacuum: both opportunities for success and structural limitations shaped the way the movement proceeded, and they also shaped the solution. The most relevant issues in analyzing the successes and shortcomings include the social movement's social composition and social location, the special nature of sterilization abuse, the choice of regulations as a strategy, and national political explanations.

The social composition of CESA and its social location structurally opened strategic possibilities while limiting other avenues. Furthermore, who the members of CESA were largely defined the resources available. The core group was composed of politically sophisticated veterans of other social and political movements, and most of them had a primary organizational connection. They were doctors, lawyers, students, health-care administrators, and political activists who were not grounded in one community, class, racial, or ethnic group.

People can best influence those institutions to which they have access. Most members of CESA had not been abused, although one had been threatened with forced sterilization when she was younger; their goal was to speak for and protect future victims. They saw the fight in the interests of all women. In a few instances, members had access to welfare, medical, and health-care institutions, serving as administrators, physicians, birth-control counselors, or social workers.

Helen Rodriguez-Trias believes that none of the reproductive rights movements are mass movements because people do not become active on that issue alone. Seen as a single issue outside the contexts of the medical-care and social-welfare systems, abuse is a specialized case. No amount of protest could change the status of those already sterilized. Unlike workers, women, renters, gays or minorities, whose social conditions can be improved as a result of their actions, there are no material incentives for the abused. Most important, their condition can not be "corrected" easily. Furthermore, it is not logical for the abused, unlike the physically disabled, for example, to desire an uplifted social status.

The nature of oppression structurally delimits the form of potential political action in two more ways. First, defiance of institutions to which people have limited access is exceedingly problematic. The only kind of social movement capable of attacking the uses of sterilization from a mass base would be an organization composed of welfare recipients, but the only active organization of welfare recipients, the National Welfare Rights Organization, has been a paper organization for years, making pronouncements without power (Piven and Cloward 1979). Second, oppression normally shapes the collectivity from which protest emerges. Abused people typically are isolated, unknown to each other, and secretive, and they sometimes feel humiliated.

Awareness of these structural limits informed CESA's strategy and philosophy. Neither CESA's will nor hard work could motivate residents of low-income and minority neighborhoods to move as some had hoped. Piven and Cloward stress that "Protest wells up in response to monumentous changes in the institutional order. It is not created by organizers and leaders" (Piven and Cloward 1979, 36). They stress, too, that insurgency and defiance happen only during periods of massive structural dislocation and change. If sterilization had been practiced in the 1960s as in the early 1970s, then an organization like the National Welfare Rights Organization could have made abuse one of its central issues. But the well had already burst, and the moment was past.

CESA thought a specific ideological sophistication and commitment were required to demystify population-control ideas and to uproot them from social policies. Neo-Malthusian ideas are the taken-for-granted, "common-sense" reality. It is easy to assert that people are hungry because there are too many mouths to feed; that families are impoverished because they have too many children; and that people cause pollution. These themes can be reduced easily to editorial cartoon depictions, simple graphics, and bumper-sticker slogans because the ideas are already deeply ingrained in American culture. Wrestling with them effectively required talking about racism, sexism, biological theories of limits, the private allocation of resources and distributional inequities, and alternative industrial organization—not exactly bumper-sticker material. Therefore, given the specific and limiting nature of the sterilization issue and the committee's understanding of population-control ideas, CESA began as and remained a small collective organization. Unlike other organizations, it eschewed organizational growth in favor of efficacy in reaching its objectives.

The specialized nature of the issue placed limitations on what was possible while providing CESA with a unique opportunity for self-education. Since sterilization was not available on a wide scale before the 1960s, no one in the United States had analyzed its potential uses and abuses. Likewise, history could not show how to mobilize opposition to the misuses of sterilization. Committees educated themselves about the issue in what they describe as exciting, dynamic, and sometimes explosive sessions. They read and discussed *The Legacy of Malthus* by Allan Chase to examine the historical linkages of population control, eugenics, and racism in the United States; *Woman's Body, Woman's Right* by Linda Gordon for a history and perspective on the relationship between efforts for reproductive rights and women's rights; and *Population Target* by Bonnie Mass to learn how and why U.S.-assisted population-control policies operate in the Third World.

A key question is not only how the social structure has limited the opportunities, but also what people did to enhance and achieve what was possible. The way in which the movement attacked abuse—through regulations—reveals much about the relationship between social composition, location, and strategy. Both the initial concern and the proposed remedy came from the ad hoc Health and Hospital Corporation (HHC) coalition, which was largely dominated by health-care administrators, lawyers, and doctors, and included community representatives. The idea of guidelines came from Esta Armstrong, who was in a position in the New York City municipal hospital system to implement and monitor guidelines, as well as to take on the chiefs of obstetrics and gynecology to ensure their enforcement. Thus the tactics of guidelines originated from the very office that would eventually be responsible for implementation and monitoring. This made it possible to achieve a working change rather than a mere paper or rhetorical victory. Furthermore, this would give the bureaucracy in charge of monitoring the regulations a stake in seeing that doctors and hospitals complied.

The institutional access, expertise, and resources available to the anti-abuse movement remained fairly constant from the original HHC regulations through the HEW campaign. Access to policy-making decisions in the medical and welfare systems was indirect at best; sometimes supporters were in positions to oversee policy and to monitor abuses. Regulations were not chosen because they promised to be the ideal solution to abuse, but because they provided one of the few strategic access points with which the movement was familiar and able to interject itself. The selection of regulations as a battleground was thus a tactical choice, perhaps the most logical one. Given the movement's identity and lack of access to institutions, regulations was the point at which it could exert the most power.

Once the strategy of guidelines was chosen, the movement's social composition and location heightened possibilities of success. Regulation campaigns allowed the movement an advantage in resources to be mobilized: CESA could not only present abused welfare mothers from different racial and ethnic backgrounds to testify, but it could also speak as experts. Counselors spoke about the lack of options, doctors talked about the practices of some of their colleagues, health care administrators lectured on enforcement, and other activists analyzed the evidence. In contrast, when representatives of the medical profession spoke they were usually on the defensive. Planned Parenthood and AVS were unaccustomed to being challenged in public on this issue, much less to having their motives scrutinized.

In an exchange of lawsuits, the advantage rested with the social movement. When abused women sued doctors and hospitals over alleged maltreatment the stories they told were often shocking and usually true, and the consequences were all the more horrifying due to their permanence. Hospitals, social-welfare agencies, and doctors defended themselves as either being misunderstood or succumbing to bureaucratic confusion. The abused, on the other hand, were presented as angry, poor, defenseless people who had been permanently damaged by powerful institutions. When the organized medical profession sued or threatened to sue it was on the more abstract basis of blunting an intended policy change. One New York City lawsuit fell apart in a manner that further discredited the medical profession's position on sterilization. Their position, as portrayed through lawsuits, drew little public sympathy.

CESA rallied an impressive spectrum of groups to its side, ranging from feminists to church groups, which reflected positively on their skills as political organizers. The committee was also effective in mobilizing public demonstrations and orchestrating public testimony on the issue at the city, state, regional, and national levels. In contrast, AVS, ACOG, and Planned Parenthood could get only themselves to testify, and then sometimes haltingly. They argued that regulations would interfere in the doctor-patient relationship and that, by limiting the immediate availability of sterilization, the women's freedom of choice would be impaired. One activist characterized Planned Parenthood's testimony on one occasion as "emotional, careless, and arrogant" (interview, unnamed respondent).

These groups appeared somewhat feeble for at least three reasons. First, they were totally unprepared to be challenged by progressives and women. Second, they not only underestimated the movement's ability to attract wide public support, but also failed to appreciate the impact such public support could have. Third, they were ambiguous about their own positions on abuse and regulations. For instance, when first asked to testify at hearings on the proposed New York City law AVS asked for a delay until it could come up with a position. The resources and skills these groups normally relied upon—money, elite status, contacts, public relations savvy—were for all practical purposes neutralized in a contest over power fought out in the public arena. The abilities to speak with authority backed by evidence, to mobilize public pressure, and to align an impressive coalition of support proved to be the superior resources and skills in this battle. After the New York City victory, one legislative assistant observed that CESA was successful because it represented no special interest, came from diverse backgrounds, and let its experience convey the depth of its conviction. CESA was described as a motley crew of "just plain folks". In contrast, the opposition was seen as well-off, professional lobbyists with axes to grind (National Women's Health Network 1980).

An additional factor hindered traditional professional birth-control organizations. Sometimes different levels of organizations are appropriately conceived as intrinsically in conflict with each other rather than mutually responsive, supportive, and consistent from top to bottom. Thus, organizations like Planned Parenthood and others delivering private services can be seen as more differentiated than their official policy declarations. This can be observed on two different levels. One is that local affiliates may have different interests, styles, and constituencies from those of their national organization. For instance, national Planned Parenthood was less vociferous in opposition to sterilization regulations than its New York branch. Karen Stamm recalls that "the affiliate and the national federation are distinctly different in their politics." The national is more "liberal" and "slicker"; in contrast the local branch "is really a lot closer to ACOG" and tends to "have the knee jerk response" (Stamm interview 1983). The second level concerns possible differences in interests between street-level workers and their agency. In Saint Louis, for example, feminist counselors at one of the largest private abortion facilities in the city wanted the agency to acknowledge that sterilization abuse was a significant problem and to support regulations. A meeting was arranged between members of CESA and the director of the agency, who acknowledged the widespread existence of sterilization abuse but felt that the agency should not support sterilization regulations because they might interfere with a woman's right to choose other services. The agency was under constant attack, and the director did not want to support anything that might jeopardize the ability to deliver abortion on demand.

Another important factor was the generally favorable media coverage of the lawsuits, hearings, and, especially, cases of abuse—an area in which CESA excelled. Differences in style between CESA and AVS, are indicative of the approaches the two sides took. AVS was highly proficient in persuading newspapers and magazines to print favorable articles about sterilization because it focused on influencing public opinion makers. CESA did not have, nor did it seek, access to publishers and editors; instead, it focused on constructing public events to put its position in the best light.

Political logic dictated both the need for a concrete contest and a victory for CESA. Regulations were selected as a strategy that could present abuse as a concrete issue and produce a victory. CESA wanted to put population-control ideas on the defensive. What they lacked in credentials and polish was compensated for by their determination, commitment, and ability to cite evidence of abuse. The other side was less sure of the issue, afraid to admit that abuse had or could take place, and failed to grasp its importance. Because of a lack of preparation and a broader sense of the issue, their normally moderate sensibilities often dissolved into the troublesome knack of arrogantly putting their feet in their mouths. One young doctor from the Indian Health Service (IHS) testified at the Kansas City Regional Hearings on the HEW regulations, no doubt more out of naiveté than maliciousness, that he was personally affronted at any suggestion of abuse among Indians at his service. Conscientious doctors like himself would never let that happen, nor could he imagine that any doctor would. Unfortunately, the sincere young doctor had just started work in an Indian Health District singled out by the general accounting office as one of the most flagrant violators of guidelines. This doctor's testimony along with others who staked the issue on their personal integrity was ridiculed. Instances of abuse tended to indict the whole system whereas testimony of professional integrity spoke only for that individual.

National political explanations were important in determining HEW's receptivity to regulations in 1978. HEW was relatively flexible on the abuse issue when confronted with a delegation from the National Conference on Sterilization Abuse. Several reasons, some of which are apparently contradictory, accounted for HEW's newfound receptiveness. A dynamic social movement had emerged to contest policy (or lack of policy) on sterilization; in large part, more stringent regulations were a concession to the anti-abuse movement. Given HEW's previous history of fumbling this volatile issue, they were only too happy to have someone suggest a workable alternative. In addition, street-level bureaucrats within HEW who were appalled at abuses and previous politicking with guidelines had their reformist positions strengthened by public pressure. According to Helen Rodriguez-Trias, another important reason for CESA's impact, and one that is contradictory to the others, "was the conservative, if not downright reactionary, climate of HEW at the time." Secretary Califano publicly admitted the presence of widespread abuse; however, some suspect an antisterilization bias was evident, reflecting the underlying religious uneasiness over sterilization (Rodriguez-Trias interview 1983).

Organizational Dilemmas

Several organizational dilemmas produced internal frictions for CESA that were important in determining how the problem of abuse was approached. One of these quandaries was whether CESA should be a core- or mass-based organization. Most in CESA felt the issue called for specialized functions and a specific ideological commitment. Sterilization was "not peoples' everyday concern, the community is not interested in this issue as a single issue," explains Karen Stamm. In analyzing the relationship between the issue and the community, she says "You can not come in from the outside and organize people to do what they themselves will not organize themselves to do." CESA could "offer support to people already there, if you have expertise. But you can't be a substitute" (Stamm interview 1983).

This approach was not without its critics. On several occasions members of CESA attempted to establish a social base anchored in a particular community, but bids to build a mass-based organization failed. Some in CESA were attracted to the possibility of organizing lower-class and minority communities around the issue of abuse. This is a classic tenet—indeed, a central orthodoxy—of radical thinking about how change will occur. Most CESA activists, however, thought it unfeasible to organize poor communities solely on this issue; instead, they reasoned that various communities, including those most likely to be potentially abused, could be mobilized periodically.

There were internal debates on whether to organize for regulations and over how much commitment and resources should be spent on such a campaign. Those opposed to regulations argued that they were merely reforms and would not promote a change in basic social relations. Others argued that regulations might provide a mask for the medical profession; that is, abuses would continue but bureaucratic regulations would make the medical profession more sophisticated, thereby making abuses harder to spot. Some argued that CESA's priorities would be altered by a preoccupation with regulations.

Karen Stamm articulates why the regulation strategy was crucial: "It is very hard to work on an issue over a long period of time where all one is doing is education work and propaganda work or research. What draws other people in, what draws the focus, is the contest over power. The regulations are a contest over power" (Stamm interview 1983). Even though there were very serious and heated discussions about the regulation strategy, most dissenters remained in CESA; however, the fight for regulations put limitations on the potential growth of the organization.

Another dilemma was that of balancing the need for coordination within a collective organization. Despite the group's insistence on collectivity, members increasingly recognized the need for overall coordination, which contradicts the organizational model. Helen Rodriguez-Trias explains that "very often you need someone who is single-minded, dedicated, super-active," but at the same time "you run into the danger of dependence on that person," the danger being that the person has "much more of an imprinting role than you wish . . . because you want to function as a collective" (Rodriguez-Trias interview 1983). Personal styles can become the pattern of the organization. Ideally, several people devoting time to coordination functions are needed, but that requires a larger organization.

Exposure of this flaw in CESA was a signal to fold up the organization. Comprehensive Employment and Training Act (CETA) monies had enabled CESA to pay a coordinator, although the "wages" were dismally low. CETA funds underwrote similar progressive organizations for several years, which helped CESA, among others, avoid the enormous task of raising funds and sustaining its own base. When CETA monies vanished CESA's day-to-day functioning depended on a worker it could no longer afford. The role the CETA worker had developed, namely, the glue of the organization, evaporated along with the money. When Helen Rodriguez-Trias went to pick up the mail, which had not been picked up in a month, fifty pounds of correspondence from around the country awaited her, and much of it required responses. Although the CETA grant had helped defray costs, it also had made CESA, like other progressive organizations, dependent on something it could neither control nor support. "It's like getting in hock for a high standard of living and then finding yourself jobless. . . . you go bankrupt," says Helen Rodriguez-Trias (interview 1983). It became obvious to her and others that it was time for CESA to fold up; they were unable to fulfill obligations and expectations, thus they could no longer consider themselves an organization.

A final organizational quandary contributing to CESA's eventual demise was the diverse commitment of its membership. Most activists brought other primary allegiances with them, which, in most cases, continued. On the one hand, different perspectives provide diversity and strength, but on the other hand, it is difficult to hang onto a secondary focus when you have a primary allegiance. CESA was a political home for only a few, while most could continue to carry out their political obligations elsewhere.

Although CESA dissolved during 1979 and 1980, work against abuse continues, and is being monitored vigilantly by other groups, such as CARASA and the Committee to Defend Reproductive Rights. The Department of Health and Human Services began a mandated review of existing regulations in 1983, and most commenting parties appear to be satisfied with the current rules. The primary opponent of the current regulations is ACOG, which opposes the rules because of the inconvenience, added expense, and loss of federal funding due to mistakes in following guidelines. Some groups would like revisions permitting more flexibility on issues like the age requirement and consent from the mentally incompetent. Abuse apparently is no longer a contested issue.

A fair assessment, given the limitations and opportunities, is that CESA won what was possible. A wholesale change in welfare policy and radically restructured health-care services—one alternative path—was not a feasible alternative in the mid-1970s. Another route would have eschewed reforms altogether to concentrate on educational or ideological concerns. In all likelihood, this route would have produced a tiny group talking to themselves and a small circle of friends.

Most important, the establishment of guidelines has been a major achievement in arresting sterilization abuse. The movement to attain administrative relief forced population-control advocates to admit the presence of coercive sterilization. The perceived success of guidelines, particularly in New York, has encouraged further efforts to reorder the doctor-patient relationship. Regulations are an important victory for those who want to change the social distribution of medical knowledge from the exclusive property of certified experts to women themselves. In 1983, HHC was in the process of proposing a contract for hysterectomies. This challenge to the traditional prerogatives of doctors and hospitals represents a step forward for health-care reformers, advocates of patients' rights, and the women's health movement.

Despite successes, the regulations have serious built-in limitations; neither the distribution of reproductive health care services nor attitudes toward public services were significantly altered. By identifying the problem as the reckless insensitivity of the medical profession and welfare policy, guidelines tend to deflect attention away from the organization and distribution of health-care services controlled by the state and whoever influences the state. Perhaps the most serious limitation of the reform is that it did not affect, nor was it intended to affect, the larger pattern of reproductive health care and sterilization in the United States. A rationalization seems to have occurred, whereby the most abusive institutional practices have been administratively remedied; there is more sensitivity to operating procedures than to a change in basic services.

Winning reforms with a single-issue, core-based movement illustrates other potential flaws. In the short run the victory in the regulations battle did not democratize public family-planning services as much as it empowered CESA as an organization and legitimated a radical and feminist critique of population control. Relying on a governmental apparatus to administratively remedy a social injustice entrusts the enforcement of that reform to a bureaucracy over which the social movement has little influence.

The federal government has provided few funds or resources for the enforcement of regulations. Department of Health and Human Services auditors report that many abuses continue with impunity. Compliance cannot be secured "because they cannot impose any penalties other than asking doctors and hospitals to repay the federal money" (cited in Petchesky 1984, 80). The threat of nonpayment has prompted ACOG to ask for changes in the rules, instead of educating doctors to change practices. This situation is no different from other state measures designed to protect the interests of consumers or the health and safety of workers against the excesses of corporations. The burden of enforcement appears to fall on those who are meant to be protected.

Lines of accountability do not run to the clientele or to the social movement, but rest within the bureaucracy itself. While it is true that not all bureaucrats or bureaucracies are insensitive to people or unresponsive to popular demands, the long-range questions of how to sustain continuous leverage and how to institutionalize monitoring remain. Reforms won through popular support can be eroded by administrative fiat or inertia. This limitation is not unique to the anti-abuse movement, but tends to be characteristic of single-issue movements in general (Murray 1982).

The state's role in delivering family-planning programs embodies many different, and opposite, elements: welfare cost cutting, population control, and the provision of essential services to those that cannot afford them. Supposing that the state will consistently and vigilantly monitor and enforce these reforms heightens the paradox of this reform. The sterilization regulations are a rare example of population politics being forced into the public arena.

NOTES

The CESA Papers is composed of several drawers of documents in the author's possession. Some of these documents were gathered during this author's participation as a CESA activist, an experience that provided the basis for some of the analytical observations here. Access to other materials was provided by various informants. The collection includes internal memos, discussion papers, minutes, action proposals, letters, leaflets, press releases, and other documents relevant to CESA's operation and the movement against abuse.

7

Population Control Politics and the Modern Welfare State

THIS EXAMINATION of population control and sterilization in the United States concludes with a discussion of population politics in the 1980s. It concludes, also, with an examination of two complex theoretical relationships as seen through the analysis of population control and sterilization: first, the functions of the modern social welfare state, and second, the configuration of class, race, and gender in American society.

Population politics in the 1980s will be bounded by three major, often interacting, structural contexts. First, changes in the family, particularly in women's roles, have generated hotly disputed issues relating to population policy. Second, transformations in the economy and labor-force requirements historically have played a dominant role in defining the issues of population-control politics. Third, the growth and development of the modern welfare state raises a number of key issues about the increasing state involvement in the lives of citizens. These distinct structural changes, which have developed in the past two to three decades, have generated "crises" that have shaped the politics of the moment. Population policy is only one aspect of a larger social and political response to these changes, and sterilization policy is but one manifestation of population policy. Family planning and immigration policy are the most visible battlegrounds in current population politics. This section frames a discussion of population policy within the context of larger societal transformations. First, one must articulate and analyze relevant trends and patterns in the family, the economy, and the state. This analysis will help to clarify the link between long-term structural changes and current population and sexual politics.

Changes in Family and Household Composition

The American family, especially the role of women, is changing profoundly. Underlying the social responses to these changes are very strong ideological currents. Making a distinction between households and families may clarify the ideological power of the notion of family. Anthropologist Rayna Rapp Reiter writes that family has at least two levels of meaning in the West: the normative nuclear family and the extended network of kin relations that people choose. Thus, *family* in America means the nuclear family plus all relations by blood and marriage. People are recruited and kept in households by families in all groups and classes; yet the families different groups and classes form are not identical because households vary in their membership and composition according to the way in which different racial, ethnic, and class groups pool and expend resources (Rapp n.d.).

The family's boundaries are continually decomposing, and reforming in constant interaction with larger economic, cultural, and historical processes. Notions of family differ both among cultures and over time within a single culture. Without seeing the family as a changing social construction—as opposed to a natural, absolute, unchanging unit—one risks assigning it to either cause or effect of social change. The size, composition, and activities of households cannot be analyzed separately from the socioeconomic relations of the society in which they are embedded. An important aspect of the way family is seen is ideological and, as such, its meaning has become a terrain of struggle. The power of the prevailing ideology about family is twofold: it uses an ahistorical concept of family to blame people for failures that are socially constructed, and it holds up a specific, white, middle-class, nuclear family with a couple of children as the model to emulate.

In 1940 women headed one in every seven American households. By 1981 they headed more than one in every four. Since 1970 the number of fatherless families has doubled (W. Bell 1983). These figures represent underlying changes in family composition and sexual behavior. Commitments to "till death do us part" are changing. Marital disruption, as measured by the divorce rate, more than doubled between 1970 and 1980. Put another way, for every 1,000 new marriages in 1960 there were 258 divorces. By 1970 this ratio rose to 328, and in 1980 it peaked at 490 before falling to 473 in 1982. Regardless of how divorces are measured, since 1960 the rate has increased to a point where there is nearly one divorce for every two marriages (Hacker 1983; *Monthly Vital Statistics Report* 1983).

Declining faith in marriage as an institution is another factor contributing to the rise in female-headed households. In 1960 three out of every ten women between the ages of twenty and twenty-four were single. In 1978 almost half of this age group had not married. At the same time, however, an estimated 1.8 million couples were living together but unmarried, more than three times as many as in 1970 (W. Bell 1983).

In 1979 a total of 597,000 children were born to unmarried mothers. In 1970 the figure was 399,000. From 1960 to 1979 the percentage of all births to mothers who were not married rose from 5.3 to 17.1 (Hacker 1983; W. Bell 1983). This steep increase is the consequence of many trends, including considerable growth in the number of teenagers who became mothers (47 percent in 1979 were not married), widespread postponement of marriage and subsequent lengthening of the years of premarital sexual life, a marked rise in the percentage of women who have experienced premarital intercourse, and teenagers' inadequate knowledge about and limited access to effective contraception (Hacker 1983; W. Bell 1983; and Petchesky 1984).

Altogether, 15,707,000 new households were created between 1970 and 1980. Of these, a little over one-half were nontraditional, such as single-person households and two or more unrelated individuals sharing living quarters. Only 22 percent of total household growth came from married couples (Hacker 1983).

Transformations in the structure and composition of the family are simultaneously the cause and consequence of a related profound structural transformation. Families with two wage earners (56 percent of two-parent families in 1979) are prevalent. The single-parent, woman-headed family is now as common as the traditional, two-parent, male-breadwinner-female-housewife family (Hacker 1983; Eisenstein 1982).

Family is a central terrain of ideological struggle; the dominant characterization of recent transformations is that the family is decaying and illegitimacy is rampant. Many people see this as a challenge to society's fundamental moral fiber; they view it as a crisis caused by a lack of moral restraint (especially sexual), women working for a wage, the intervention of the welfare state, and the pernicious influence of feminism. This interpretation of the crisis in American families clearly suggests parameters for family and population policy. Broadly defined, social policy should aim to strengthen blood ties, stabilize marriages, encourage small families, and build up the "feminine" sphere within the family; practically, this translates into condemning illegitimacy, frowning upon female-headed families and nuclear families with large numbers of children, lessening rewards for wage-earning women, and discouraging non-nuclear households while strengthening the male-headed, two-parent family. Mechanisms for achieving this range from the ideological to state-sponsored coercion, from the preaching of evangelists to loss of social benefits. The current debate over the family is uneven—it is dominated by the New Right, neoconservatives, and antifeminists. Until the basis of the debate is effectively challenged the crisis of the family will remain defined the way it is. Proposed solutions will follow the New Right's logic, no matter what phenomena underlie recent changes. Therefore, reactive and conservative proposals for population and family policy probably will be compatible with population-control objectives.

Changes in the Economy and Employment Patterns

Between 1970 and 1980 the number of people working in the United States increased from 78 to 97 million. In a period of economic stagnation 18.5 million new jobs were created, which is equivalent to the entire working population of Poland. Changes in the occupational structure reflect trends that have been developing for a generation. The most striking trend is a shift away from industrially based employment, toward growth in the service and retail sectors. While the United States is far from becoming either a post-industrial society or an industrial weakling, these trends indicate the diminishing significance of an industrial occupational structure.

Employment patterns have shifted in the economic marketplace. Between 1970 and 1980 most new jobs were for secretaries, followed by cashiers, nurses, dieticians, and therapists. New jobs were concentrated in two sectors of the private economy—services and retail trade—which provided more than 70 percent of all new private jobs created from 1973 to 1980 (Rothschild 1981). This signifies that "waiting on tables, defrosting frozen hamburgers, rendering 'services to buildings,' looking after the old and the ill . . . [are] women's work" (Rothschild 1981, 12–13). Women's participation in the labor force is vital both to the growth of these sectors and to family maintenance.

Recent job growth is generally in the secondary labor market, where occupations are dominated by women. Employment in this sector tends to be part-time or seasonal, with subsistence-level wages, few fringe benefits (such as health care), and limited promotional opportunities. In the early 1970s, about 40 percent of women heading welfare families worked at some point during the year. The need for welfare to supplement low-paying, underutilized, dead-end labor is obvious (Erie, Rein, and Wiget 1982).

Women's entry into the labor force has been impressive: 23 million worked in 1960, 31.5 million in 1970, and 44.6 million by 1980. In 1960 the labor force was 33.4 percent women, but by 1980 women accounted for 42.4 percent of the paid workforce. According to a *New York Times* poll conducted in November 1983, only 33 percent of women currently working for a wage would prefer to return home and take care of house and family (*New York Times* 1983). This varies by income and occupation: only 27 percent of high income earning professionals want to return home, whereas 49 percent of women in blue-collar jobs would rather be home. Although jobs offer increased independence, fulfillment, creativity, and a sense of self-worth for many, the reality for most women is that work is essential to their survival and that of their families, both of which are difficult to maintain on a single wage.

Zillah Eisenstein calls attention to the connection between changes in family life and employment patterns.

> The private sector growth reflects the market's response to changes in the family, as well as changes in the relation between state and the family. Increases in state welfare services, nursing homes, and fast food restaurants all reflect new trends in family life, particularly the changes in woman's place within the family *and* within the market [Eisenstein 1982, 89].

The expansion of employment in eating and drinking establishments, for instance, is closely connected to persistent long-term trends in family and household composition: those living alone are more likely to eat out, and families with working women spend more money eating out.

The much-touted high technology revolution reveals another dimension of the new employment trend. According to a study commissioned by *Business Week*, high technology in the next decade will give birth to fewer than one million jobs, two-thirds of which will be in traditionally clerical or operative occupations.

A recent study clarifies the high-tech strategy for growth. Between 1978 and 1990, the United States will need three times as many new janitors and maintenance personnel (600,000) as new systems analysts (150,000). New jobs for computer programmers (150,000) will be less than one-fifth the projected growth for fast-food workers and kitchen helpers (800,000) (Shorrock 1983). Between 1980 and 1990, the Department of Labor projects that most new jobs will continue to be generated in generally low-paying occupations, such as secretaries, nurses' aids, janitors, sales clerks, and cashiers (*New York Times* 1983).

Masked by the tremendous growth in new jobs in the last decade and hastened by the Reagan recession are permanent consequences from these structural changes. Almost eight million families fell out of the middle-class earning range (families making between $17,000 and $41,000) between 1979 and 1983. Between 1972 and 1982 real family income was depressed by more than 8 percent (Harrington 1984). No matter how broad an industrial boom, the traditional industrial employment base will not recover fully. A gradual but persistent trend is the shift to service employment, which is highly concentrated and predominantly female; McDonalds now employs more workers than U.S. Steel.

This structural transformation carries a clear implication for population policy: continued population expansion is no longer required to sustain economic growth and profitability. What was a constant American premise from Colonial days through the boom of the 1960s is no longer valid. Cheap, mobile labor is no longer needed to go to the factories because the factories can now go to the cheap labor (e.g., South Korea, Taiwan, Mexico, etc.).

Changes in the State's Role in Social Well-Being

The third major context contributing to the make up of population policy is the government's involvement in the social well-being of its citizens. In 1950 public social-welfare programs cost $23.5 billion; by 1979 these costs had risen to $428.3 billion. Social welfare is expensive, and in the United States these costs have soared. Between 1975 and 1979 alone, due to the severe economic recession and soaring inflation, public expenditures were pushed from $290 to $428 billion. These expenditures increased 103.7 percent from 1970 to 1979, adjusted for inflation. Social welfare's rising cost represents a transformation in its share of American productivity and of total public spending. In 1950 social-welfare costs were the equivalent of 8.9 percent of the gross national product (GNP). By 1970 they represented 15.2 percent of GNP, 40.1 percent of the federal budget, and 48.2 percent of the outlays of governments at all levels. By 1979 these social expenditures had increased to 18.5 percent of GNP, 55 percent of federal costs, and 56.8 percent of all governmental costs.

The lion's share of increases since 1975 has gone for new social-security beneficiaries and medical and hospital costs. Overall, the largest category is social insurance, followed by education expenses; these two categories accounted for almost two-thirds of all social welfare costs in the United States. The third largest item is health programs, and public aid ranks fourth. In 1979 public aid amounted to just 9 percent of the total investment in public social welfare (W. Bell 1983).

Of each $1,000 in transfer payments, $858 went for pension or disability payments. Hostility, nonetheless, is directed mainly against what is commonly called "welfare"; that is, Aid to Families with Dependent Children (AFDC) and programs for the needy. AFDC, food stamps, and child nutrition programs have increased. From 1961 to 1979 AFDC families headed by women more than quadrupled, from 635,000 to 3,000,000. Piven and Cloward argue that these increases have been largely a response to the urban unrest of the 1960s and the social movement among the poor in the early 1970s (Piven and Cloward 1982). One Malthusian misconception is that the poor have much higher birth rates; welfare recipients are accused of begetting more children to secure more public welfare. "There is no question that many well-intended Great Society type programs contributed to . . . a large increase in births out of wedlock," President Reagan said in his weekly radio address of December 3, 1983 (*New York Times*). The facts are different.

The welfare state has become increasingly intertwined with the fortunes of working women. Reciprocal changes in household structures, work structures, and welfare policy have been integral factors in what is being called the "feminization of poverty." That over half the nation's female-headed families were receiving AFDC in 1979 does not reflect a liberalization of eligibility requirements, but rather a general rise in poverty coupled with a shift in who the poor are. In the ten-year period from 1969 to 1979, the number of female-headed families living in poverty rose up from 1.8 to 2.6 million. Meanwhile, the number of male-headed families living in poverty dipped steadily through the same period, declining from 3.2 to 2.7 million. From 1959 to 1979 the proportion of all low-income families headed by women dramatically increased from 23 to 48 percent. Erie, Rein, and Wiget (1982) argue that federal and state welfare policy amount to a de facto labor policy for women in the secondary labor market; if they are correct, then social policies have helped to increase the impoverishment of women.

The dollars spent on social welfare reflect a deepening state penetration into what previously had been private spheres of social life—child care, child nutrition, social insurance, housing, nursing homes, and birth control. Concomitant with this penetration, as the accepted misperception goes, is an army of social regulators, do-gooders and other federal bureaucrats. From 1952 to 1982 total employment at all levels of government rose 137 percent; employment at the federal level, however, increased only 9 percent. The bulk of the increases occurred at the state and local levels (U.S. Office of Management and Budget 1983). Moreover, the federal share of the total public payroll has been declining consistently since 1952; the ratio of federal employees per 10,000 people also has been declining; and federal employees represented a smaller portion of the total workforce in 1981 than in 1955 (U.S. Bureau of the Census 1981).

Another common misperception is that growth in social expenditures (assumed to mean payments to the poor) and in the federal bureaucracy is wildly out of control, having attained a life of its own. The problem, therefore, is commonly defined as a burgeoning state sector, widespread state penetration into private spheres, and out-of-control federal budgets spurred by welfare costs—all of which are seen as prime contributors to public deficit spending and the state's fiscal crisis. Against the backdrop of occupation transitions, high levels of unemployment, and fiscal crises of the federal government and cities, social-welfare expenditures have become a prime target of cost controls. Population restrictions may have appeal in the context of reducing long-term welfare costs by reducing the growth of a permanent underclass.

Increases in social-welfare spending have been immense. Yet, among the eighteen industrialized capitalist nations, the United States ranks fourteenth in share of gross domestic product devoted to social welfare (W. Bell 1983). This increase is the result of a maturing social insurance system, soaring medical costs, education commitments, inflationary spirals, and programs to assist the poor.

Notwithstanding a separation of fact from cultural fiction, slogans alluding to "welfare reform," sending the bureaucrats packing, and getting the government out of citizens' private lives clearly define the crises arising from the state's role in social well-being. There is a twist to the state's penetration. As the welfare state breaches the barrier between public responsibility and private affairs, it becomes more legitimate and better able to apply population policy and to respond to calls for population control to contain costs.

In the absence of alternative explanations and a viable progressive movement, the social panorama emerging from the transformations in the family, the economy, and the role of the state has profoundly conservative implications for population policy. These three transformations can be described separately, but they are related dialectically and the effects may be synergistic. Each transformation presupposes another; thus the implications they have for population policy as a whole are distinguished only by the gestalt of all three taken together.

The crucial question for population policy asks what kinds of policies are shaped by the current mode of capital accumulation and corporate strategy, by the family crisis, and by the welfare crisis. In short, there is no longer a necessity to reproduce a growing labor force. In previous eras, this labor requirement was taken for granted; absorbing the social costs of reproducing and training, along with cyclical unemployment, was considered legitimate by most businessmen. Now, however, the diminished need for an expanding labor force coupled with a fiscal crisis has reversed the onus for most businessmen, and they believe that population growth leads to excessive social costs; an exacerbation of welfare, environmental, urban, resource, and infrastructure problems; and, ultimately, social unrest. Thus the burden has shifted structurally and politically. Those who see the family crisis springing from illegitimacy (especially among the poor and minorities), the breakdown of patriarchy, and federal intervention in family life opt for population policies that limit growth. Those who see the welfare "mess" as either fiscally intolerable or rewarding a breakdown of traditional family life favor restrictive population policies. Consistencies are not ironclad, however, because growth in retail and service sectors is fueled by a large pool of unorganized and low-paid women who must work to support themselves and their families. In addition, differences and divisive issues exist among the current political actors. These transformations have repercussions in many areas of American life and politics; most important here is their effect on population politics and policy.

The positions of Malthus, the Neo-Malthusians, and the women's movement are embodied in contemporary population politics. The New Right carries forth the Malthusian legacy; the neoconservatives, population-control groups, family-planning professionals, and the capitalist class generally follow the Neo-Malthusian line; and the women's movement focuses on women's reproductive health and control over their own bodies. An analysis of these positions demonstrates that potential conflicts and shifting alliances threaten the current balance of forces. Two issues that were previously analyzed generate contradictory positions. The first is the issue of women in the labor force, which places the New Right at odds with the corporations and the women's movement. The mutually reinforcing systems of patriarchy and capitalism conflict on this issue. The enormous growth of the retail and service sectors has been predicated on the entry of women into the labor market and the consequent need to purchase domestic services outside the home. According to the New Right's logic, married women who work for a wage corrode the bonds of patriarchy and the social stability provided by the nuclear family; working wives also undermine women's specialness. The women's movement, in sharp contrast, heralds women's participation at all levels of society while being particularly watchful of equality in occupational opportunities and wages. On this issue there seems to be a clear distinction between the Malthusians on the one side and the Neo-Malthusians on the other. One line of speculation is that with high levels of structural unemployment, a stabilizing influence might be to dislodge women from some occupations and replace them with men whose jobs have been liquidated technologically; however, this would take a more prodigious effort than the one that attempted to return "Rosie the Riveter" to the kitchen. Women's labor-force participation is an issue that potentially separates the New Right from its corporate supporters.

The second issue that generates conflict, the state's role in providing reproductive-health and contraceptive services, is battling about sex education, abortion rights, teen-age counseling and family-planning services, thus pitting the New Right versus the women's movement. Population-control and family-planning groups believe their goal can be executed most effectively and humanely through the assistance of the welfare state. If, however, the moral repression of the New Right is successful, then some of the orthodox population-control groups may relinquish or reduce their commitment to family-planning services. Although this is true for population-control groups whose primary concern is overpopulation among the poor and minorities, it may not be so for groups dedicated to freedom-of-choice issues. Feminists are working more closely with organizations like Planned Parenthood because they are targets of the same New Right attack, and hence they are potential allies. The problem is distinguishing whether Planned Parenthood's interest in freedom-of-choice issues is a tactical response or whether the organization sees vital principles at stake. Given Planned Parenthood's history, the belief that some parts of the organization are motivated by principles (street-level workers and volunteers, some of its local affiliates and national leadership), and the suspicion of the feminist and women's health movements, such a distinction cannot be cleanly drawn. The fragile coalition that has formed is marked by considerable uneasiness on all sides. But if the message of moral repression is effective, then financial and political support for groups like Planned Parenthood will be less generous.

The new right and the women's movement will argue vociferously over family and sexual politics. The primary arbiter will be the corporate interests that, in this situation, have always held the key leverage. As a crucial part of their long-term strategy to accumulate greater profits, they benefit by reducing social services, with income-maintenance programs taking the brunt of the assault. Since World War II, as demonstrated by the Population Council, this dominant group has recognized that its interests are served by state-assisted population-control programs. In the 1980s, however, the dominant corporate interests have begun to identify with the neoconservative and New Right ideological solutions to rising social expenditures. It may be politically expedient for corporate leaders to go along with attacks on *all* welfare programs, consenting to cutbacks in family-planning services in the process.

Social-welfare programs serve the larger political, economic, and social objectives as defined by the corporate elite and the wealthy. In the past they have supported state-sponsored family-planning services, especially insofar as these programs are influenced by population-control objectives. It will take the mobilization of extraordinary political energies for welfare policy to change and reflect a position more in tune with clients' needs.

An Alternative View

Current population and sexual politics are dominated by perceptions of reality that conceal rather than reveal social reality, for example, the *prevailing* interpretations of transformations in the economy, family, and role of the state. In turn, implications for population policies are premised on these flimsy interpretations. In all three spheres, data indicate persuasively that important structural shifts and changes are occurring. Precisely what has given rise to these changes and what social implications they may signify, however, is something substantially different from what is indicated by the contemporary political debate.

There is little disagreement that the American economy has declined with respect to its past performance and to other capitalist nations. Changing employment patterns—shifting of jobs and rising unemployment—are visible parts of the response to this decline. The American economy began to decline for many reasons: American companies became complacent about the need to modernize their domestic facilities, investing instead in more profitable sectors and regions; the American government acceded to the immediate needs of business, neglecting longer-term priorities; economic ascendency occurred in other capitalist nations; and American foreign policy goals created a heavy burden on industry.

Underlying this are changes in the international economy, and in America's role in international relations. The immensely profitable postwar boom has ended because the conditions that made it possible no longer exist. American corporations have responded by moving away from investments in productive capacity that would generate stable employment and higher living standards, but are less profitable; instead, their strategy favors more profitable overseas investments and speculation. Corporations have responded to the challenge from Japan and other countries by closing American plants and reopening them in Asia and Latin America where labor is cheap, unions are weaker, environmental and safety laws are nonexistent, and governments are friendly to foreign investors (Bluestone and Harrison 1982; Magaziner and Reich 1982; Piven and Cloward 1982). These strategies have profound implications for the industrial capacity of the United States and, most important in terms of understanding the structural dynamics of population policies, for the types and patterns of employment they generate. An economic blueprint that devalues industrial production in the United States features population limitation as an appealing byproduct.

What some people cite as statistics of doom could be signals of liberation (i.e., some of the changes in household and family composition). The family is largely understood as a harmonious and private institution, a refuge from the violence, conflict, and mass impersonal character of the larger society, but itself the cradle of love and intimacy. Recently, this idyllic portrait has been challenged. It is an adjustment that points to the family as often being a "cradle of violence," which legitimates and makes socially acceptable the use of violence in child rearing and in the society at large. Researchers have documented that the family is also a place where violence and hate are felt, expressed, and learned (Breines and Gordon 1983; Gelles 1979; Steinmetz and Straus 1974).

This powerful critique places the rising trends of divorce, separation, single-mother households, premarital sexual activity, communal living, and homosexual pairing in a very different light. Some of these moves away from traditional two-parent, lifelong commitments may be flights from male domination, patriarchy, and rigidly defined sexuality. Escape from violent forms of male domination and repression, such as wife beating, child beating, sexual abuse and incest, can be seen as recognition of the need for something better. Although most changes in family structure may occur for other reasons, many new family and household forms reflect a conscious and sometimes desperate search for something other than oppressive patriarchal structures undergirded by social norms, economic dependence, and physical force. Virginia Woolf (1966, 74) captures the double bind women face when they exchange traditional roles for "modern" ones, thus getting caught between "the devil and the deep sea. Behind us lies the patriarchal system; the private house with its nullity, its immorality, its hypocrisy, its servility. Before us lies the public world, the professional system, with its possessiveness, its pugnacity, its greed."

An unspecifiable amount of "illegitimacy," especially among teenagers, results less from moral laxity or stupidity than from a larger set of transformations. Early marriage as the defining objective in women's lives is being rejected in an expectation of economic independence. This can be seen in the declining number of first pregnancies legitimated through marriage: among white girls aged fifteen to nineteen, such legitimations fell steeply from 51 percent in 1971 to 20 percent in 1979 (Petchesky 1984). Kristin Luker (1975) observes that many young women become pregnant not out of ignorance or lack of access to contraception, but because contraceptive planning signals an image of "looseness" or "availability" that they want to avoid. Inadequate knowledge about reproduction and contraception coupled with unavailable services swells the ranks of unwed mothers. Given that the unemployment rate among minority youth is nearly 40 percent and that women with little or no education are especially disadvantaged in the labor market, childbearing may take on different meanings to poor women, many of whom see it as the only meaningful adult role open to them. In addition, children can provide a sense of satisfaction and achievement.

Finally, the spread of social-welfare services can be put in a different perspective. Income-maintenance programs, established in the 1930s and 1960s, today provide a minimal maintenance level for disabled, elderly, unemployed, and other poor people. This represents an encroaching democratization of an important part of the economic sphere. The strategy of business and the state is to squeeze inflation by putting millions out of work and by reducing the standard of living for still millions more. In other words, if the health of the economy depends on massive unemployment and reduced standards of living, then the victims of this strategy, the new poor, will seek relief. The rise in welfare spending also can be seen as the state's answer to changes in the family and to women's entry into the labor market.

Piven and Cloward (1982) argue that Reagan and his big-business allies launched a sudden and massive attack on federal entitlement programs so that workers receiving benefits would be forced back into the labor market, thereby depressing wages and increasing business profits. They maintain that the expansion of federal income maintenance in the late 1960s and early 1970s increased the bargaining power of workers by giving them extra-market means of subsistence, thus reducing their need to enter the labor market during periods of high unemployment. The current attack on welfare, which may reflect intent to remove this "cushion," has another important dimension; as Erie, Rein, and Wiget (1982) point out, the attack is also being aimed at the new classes benefiting from the expanded welfare state—the poor and those servicing them, largely women in both cases.

These alternative views of the crisis are merely sketched here; nonetheless, in broad outline, a critical perspective on patriarchy and corporate capitalism will yield interpretations vastly different from current ones, which are premised on undiluted defenses of patriarchy and corporate capitalism.

Inherent in this critical perspective is the assumption that the dynamics of population growth, particularly for the poor, should not be treated as an isolated, independent factor to be manipulated by the state at the behest and convenience of the wealthy and powerful.

Connected to this critical approach is a very different perspective on population policy. It should be recognized that in this period of American history there are compelling reasons to prefer a lower growth rate to a higher one. The problem, seen from a critical perspective, is how to encourage this in a democratic manner. Family health-care programs must encompass the spectrum of reproductive health-care—including maternal health-care, reproductive and contraceptive education, and sterilization—and incorporate an emphasis on quality of services. Ideally, programs would be women-centered, and operating procedures would be subject to community review. Last, population policy in conjunction with other relevant objectives should be linked primarily to overall quality, improving the position of women and producing opportunities for better conditions of life.

Reproductive Services, Motherhood, and the Modern Welfare State

This study of the role of sterilization as part of population-control policies raises theoretical questions about the role of the modern welfare state and the intricate connections among class, race, and gender. Population-control politics clarifies some of the important issues.

Historical and cross-cultural comparisons can help locate and illuminate present-day actions. In Nazi Germany, pronatalism for desirable births and antinatalism for undesirable ones were connected. Two laws prohibited the availability of abortion facilities and services. Doctors and nurses were obliged to inform state authorities of all miscarriages so the police could investigate for suspected abortion. Healthy Aryan women were exhorted to bear children for the greater glory of country and race (Bock 1983). The laws were strictly enforced, as almost seven thousand people were convicted for violating the anti-abortion law between 1932 and 1938.

The other side of the policy was race hygienic sterilization. In 1933 a law was passed against propagating "lives unworthy of life," which ordered sterilizations for certain categories of people, even prescribing the use of force against those who did not submit voluntarily. Compulsory motherhood and prohibition of motherhood were two sides of Nazi body politics (Bock 1983).

During the emergency rule imposed on India from 1975 to 1977, Indira Gandhi's government was accused of forcing sterilization on villagers, mostly men, who were rounded up and taken to camps where vasectomies were performed. In some of the campaigns, men and women were offered money or radios as an incentive to "volunteer." Although done for different purposes—race hygiene in Germany, overpopulation in India—the state in both instances resorted to Draconian measures to implement population-control policies.

In the United States, people as diverse as Margaret Sanger, H. L. Mencken, and William Shockley have suggested sterilization bonus schemes, with inducement by monetary incentives. This position is a giant step away from the compulsory state-directed solutions of Germany and India; it is also different in that the state never embraced the scheme.

The power of the modern welfare state can be used to oppress or liberate, or to do both simultaneously. Policy outcomes are not mandated through camps, decrees, or bonus schemes. Instead, a highly sophisticated corporate and administrative rationality, an ideology of equality of opportunity, and the constraints of agencies delivering public services combine to shape the desired results. One of the central features marking the emergence of a corporate liberal structure in the United States is that the nature of control (in the marketplace, labor discipline, or social control generally) changes from raw individual power to that of administrated, rationalistic, bureaucratic power (Edwards 1979; Schirmer 1982). The state becomes more responsible for preserving the mode of production, for planning, for economic coordination, and for allocating resources. The key to understanding social welfare is in the functions it serves for the larger economic, social, and political order (Piven and Cloward 1971). Seen in this perspective, maintaining gender hierarchy and regulating family life are a concern of the state. Elizabeth Wilson (1977, 9) argues that welfare state policies amount to a set of ideas about society, the family, and women—the "State organization of domestic life." The actual giving of relief or services is seen as a concession or as a supportive institution.

An ideology of equality allows the state to acknowledge the need for and to provide family-planning services. It is important to note that an unmistakably progressive element of the social welfare state is reinforced because there is a real need for services and in one sense the state is responding to articulated needs. Undoubtedly, millions of women have benefited from these services, but they are selective and the choices are patterned by the narrow social constraints in which they are offered.

Choices are socially structured by three mechanisms. First, decisions about reproductive health are influenced by the kinds of social services generally available. While the ideology of equality may operate for family planning, it is not as evident in areas supportive of child rearing. Cuts in day-care centers; school lunch programs; welfare eligibility and allotments; the women, infant and children nutritional program; and other restrictions mitigate against raising large families. The state makes it easier for a mother on welfare to obtain a sterilization than to keep warm in winter, find child care, or provide nourishing meals for her children. Second, the choices available for clients using publicly funded services are restricted in relation to those readily available for the rest of the society. The relationship between the drastically reduced availability of abortion and the increased numbers of sterilization for the poor attests to this dynamic: between 1977 and 1981 Medicaid sterilizations rose from 72,300 to 97,300; in contrast, federally financed abortions plummeted from 300,000 to 18,000 as a result of the Hyde Amendment. Third, the presentation of birth-control information and options and the delivery of these services by medical and welfare personnel patterns choices within the already limited context of what is possible. Bureaucratic dynamics result in a skewing of choices toward longer-lasting or permanent services.

Family planning, particularly in sterilization, thus reflects a duality in the social-welfare state. There is a simultaneous tendency for family-planning services to be both progressive and coercive, to acknowledge and provide needed services, but within a social context that obliges clients to conform to rules offering restricted choices and prescribed options (Gough 1979; Schirmer 1982). Human welfare is enhanced and negated in the same process.

Finally, for those sterilized, the act tends to validate and internalize a conception of being economically powerless, sexually irresponsible, and socially inadequate. Many women who see themselves as victims of sterilization have not publicly vocalized their dissatisfaction; because they are isolated from others who feel as they do, they are politically indifferent. The public was informed— and many were outraged—about blatant coercive sterilization, and a social movement sprang up in response. In contrast, the workings of the rationalistic social-welfare state may have precluded a similar awareness and action about discriminatory patterns of sterilization. Unlike other felt injustices, sterilization is an issue on which those regretting their patterned choice are not likely to launch a public campaign.

Lipsky outlines some of the broader social control functions of the modern welfare state. Public social services play a crucial part "in softening the impact of the economic system on those who are not its primary beneficiaries and inducing people to accept the neglect or inadequacy of primary economic and social institutions" (Lipsky 1980, 11). The extension of the welfare state also represents an expanding terrain of social control. Nowhere is this dynamic clearer than in reproductive services. State policies of fertility, population, and sexual control are attempts to impose public purposes over the core of social life.

The modern welfare state helps to reproduce prevailing social values of the larger society. The general stigmatization of poor people provides subtle justification for policies and patterns of practice that result in institutionalized discrimination. The dependency and subordination of welfare clients is confirmed by bureaucratic control that, in turn, affects recipients' self-respect and expectations.

Social-service agencies mediate conflict between poor citizens and the state. Frustration at inequities of opportunities and distribution may be understood by clients as personal malfeasance by social-service personnel or doctors. This mediation structures conflict in several ways; most important, it deflects attention away from the system and focuses on change in attitudes, training, routines, and procedures of public agencies. Through social-welfare agencies society organizes the control, restriction, and maintenance of relatively powerless groups. Antagonism is directed toward the agents of social services and control and away from political forces that ultimately account for the distribution of social and material values. Lipsky (1980, 188) succinctly states the ramifications for change: "If bureaucracies mirror the society in which they develop it is difficult to change bureaucratic forms fundamentally without larger changes taking place."

The same negative attitudes, policies, and practices used to dissuade certain women from procreating sanction childbearing for others. Woman's role in patriarchy to wed, to create an orderly and supportive household for husband and children, and to accept dependency on the breadwinner is symbolically "rewarded" with positive attitudes toward procreation and a few, although inconsistent and dwindling, pro-natalist policies. The right to bear children is not absolute but is socially conditioned by women's relationship to men and by marriage and class. The state attempts to regulate the terms of family life.

The modern welfare state reflects and perpetuates two different, though connected, norms for children. Children are seen as evidence of a successful negotiation of female roles within the patriarchal family. For those without support and on welfare, children are seen as public burdens and perhaps as signs of irresponsibility and failure. These women should cease procreating and, if failing to find suitable husbands, should find jobs instead.

Practices are not just subtle ads for patriarchy; they are aggressively sexist as well. While 53 percent of those sterilized nationwide are women, 98 percent of the sterilizations financed by Medicaid are performed on women. It is true that since men do not need reproductive health care they are not caught up in the same institutional net. Yet the far riskier wholesale practice of sterilizing women and not men also results from women bearing the major responsibility for contraception and from isolating reproductive health care and making it more accessible.

In much the same way that patriarchy is socially sanctioned and reinforced by welfare policy, so too are class differences—in this case especially the division between those who are assisted by the welfare state and those who are not. Procreation is discouraged not only when women are without husbands or have too many children, but also when their economic standing is inferior. The social control onus is to prevent pregnancy. It should be remembered that family planning *must* be available for AFDC clients. The barrage of formal and informal messages say not to have children—a very different message from the one given to women of "superior" classes. While this dual message about childbearing is most decipherable on a welfare versus nonwelfare basis, it also applies to the poor more generally as a class of people.

The theoretical complexities of class, race, and gender in the case of population control and sterilization can be seen in the intricate links among all three. Women receiving public assistance are the primary targets of a sexist, class-based population-control perspective that, through the state, attempts to limit their procreation. Thus the modern welfare state provides services while sanctioning who can and cannot bear children, artificially dividing women and validating class divisions.

Drawing rigid theoretical formulations about the nature of social control and the modern welfare state would be premature. This examination of the politics of fertility control provides compelling grounds for caution in presuming that the welfare state is either totally monolithic or omnipotent. It cannot be portrayed as monolithic because policies and programs vary both among states and within a state. The New Federalism provides individual states with more latitude to set levels of service and to spend federal money on programs as it sees fit. For example, abortion and sterilization rates vary among regions and states, proving that federal policies can be perceived and applied unevenly and that local influences play a role. When Medicaid abortions were defunded several states responded by providing their own funding. At the behest of organized social movements, states, such as California and New York, adopted more stringent sterilization regulations than those set by the federal government, effectively prodding the welfare state to review its own regulations and approve more protective ones. This demonstrates that the dominant structural position of corporate interests and medical monopolies does not exclusively determine every health and welfare policy. At various times and on specific issues, however, popular practices, changing ideologies, organized social movements, and corporate rationalizers play important roles, even though the dominant structural interests remain the preponderant power over basic policy objectives.

Women in all cultures have consciously attempted to regulate their fertility, making methods of fertility control an important part of their collective experience and culture. Women have not been obliging, passive recipients of whatever the state or men deem wise. Conceptually, it is more accurate to view the welfare state as responding to popular practices, social conditions, and changing ideologies about sexuality and family. The pressing need and desire to control fertility has been the source of many struggles for women, and it is a key thread in the women's movement. The reactive stance of the welfare state to repress or to dictate the ways in which fertility can be regulated has not worked historically. The Comstock Law of 1873 and the Hyde Amendment a little over a hundred years later have failed to abolish the practice and use of abortion, although these anti-abortion efforts have altered drastically the social conditions under which abortion occurs. Thus the state is not omnipotent; it is often defied openly.

The trend to "medicalize" fertility control by technological means contains a promise and a threat. The promise is safer, healthier, and more effective methods of birth control. Foundations, government agencies, and pharmaceutical companies sponsoring contraceptive research could have chosen to address the question of developing methods centered on and controlled by women rather than the professional-dependent methods that ultimately became the basis of the contraceptive revolution. The alternatives were probably not even imagined. Technology threatens to replace women's knowledge and control with drugs and devices designed, controlled, and supervised by experts and commercial interests. The normal application of contraceptive technology contains significant consequences because many women are routinely forced to choose hazardous drugs and devices like the IUD, sterilization, and Depo-Provera. This scientific management approach to fertility regulation has not deprived women the wisdom of centuries of tradition and knowledge. Feminist health centers consciously emphasize women's knowledge of their own bodies and women-centered and women-controlled methods like the cervical cap.

Sophisticated and professional-dependent medical technologies, such as sterilization or Depo-Provera, in the hands of scientists and physicians strengthens their professional monopoly, increasing the differential in power between them and their patients. When the patient is on welfare, the social-control dimension is further strengthened: the more sophisticated the technology, the greater the potential for social control and abuse. The more radical or permanent the method is, the more effective the results are likely to be. Sterilization can be used to liberate women from the burdens of birth-control worries, but for many on welfare it is a social control mechanism, the appropriate technology to induce a limited population growth among that class of women.

This contraceptive technology is also part of the social constellation that ushered in the "sexual revolution" and shaped new norms about sexuality and the exploitation of sexuality. Whether or not one finds these changes liberating or reprehensible, a consequence of the sexual revolution is greater reliance on contraceptive drugs and devices, some of which are hazardous.

The welfare state may have planted its own seeds of change. The deeper it penetrates private spheres of social life, the more vulnerable government becomes to challenges based on improving the quality of life and social equality. Thus the modern welfare state, in rhetorically justifying its increasing penetration of private life, contains elements that contradict the control it presumably exerts. Once the fiscal and ideological commitment to reproductive health care is made, these programs become vulnerable to demands for change that are based on taking the idea of equality of opportunity seriously. The rhetoric hints at inherent possibilities and potentially unleashes aspirations for reproductive freedom, social justice, and equality.

Too often in the past the success of population-control politics depended finally on the inability of the American people to see through the mystification of Malthusianism. Too frequently, the politics of fertility control were substituted for social reform and allowed to operate without public understanding. The dominance of population control has depended ultimately on acquiescence of Americans to the combined power of state policies and an ideology received from the past. These legacies have been instrumental in preventing modern methods of birth control from being utilized fully in the long struggles for reproductive freedom, sexual equality, and social justice. Instead, population control attempts to usurp the fullest possibilities of present technology and to turn them into their opposite. The potentials of modern birth-control technology will only be realized if sexual equality, social justice, and reproductive freedom become integral parts of a sweeping movement for social change so that people, especially women, are not manipulated by those who control the technology, but guide their own destiny.

In 1972 when Mary Alice, age twelve, and Minnie Relf, age fourteen, were spirited away by a family-planning nurse to be sterilized, their older sister Kate locked herself in her room to avoid the same fate. If the instincts of a sixteen-year-old girl can cut through decades of propaganda, ideology, and mystification, then there is hope.

Appendix

Groups Represented at the National Conference on Sterilization Abuse

Ad Hoc Women's Studies Group Against Sterilization Abuse

American Baptist Churches

American Baptist Indian Caucus

American Citizens Concerned for Life

American Friends Service Committee

Association for Voluntary Sterilization

Bay Area American Indians

Center for Constitutional Rights

Committee for Abortion Reform and Against Sterilization Abuse

Christian Church

Committee to End Sterilization Abuse, Boston

Committee to End Sterilization Abuse, New York

Committee to End Sterilization Abuse, Saint Louis

Committee to End Sterilization Abuse, Western Massachusetts

Feminist Women's Health Center, Atlanta

Feminist Women's Health Center, Chicago

Feminist Women's Health Center, Los Angeles

Feminist Women's Health Center, Tallahassee

Friends Committee

Institute for the Development of Indian Law

Interreligious Foundation for Community Organization

Latin Women's Collective

National Abortion Rights Action League

National Council of Churches

National Council of Negro Women

National Indian Youth Council

National Organization for Women

National Urban League

National Welfare Rights Organization, New York

Native American News Service

Native American Solidarity Committee

Northern Cheyenne Land Owners Association

People for Choice on Abortion and Sterilization

Planned Parenthood Federation of America

Public Advocate

Off Our Backs

Senate Committee on Indian Affairs

Southwestern Indian Development

Sterilization and Informed Consent Rights

Third World Newsreel

United Church of Christ

United Methodist Church

United Presbyterian Church

Women Against Sterilization Abuse

Women's Action Project

Women's Bureau, Department of Labor

Young Women's Christian Association

References

Ad Hoc Advisory Committee on Sterilization Guidelines. 1975. Why Sterilization Guidelines Are Needed. Mimeograph.

Alford, Robert. 1975. *Health Care Politics*. Chicago: University of Chicago Press.

Allen, Garland. 1975. Genetics, Eugenics and Class Struggle. *Genetics* 79 (June): 29–45.

Allen, Garland, and Barry Mehler. 1977. Sources in the Study of Eugenics #1: Inventory of the American Eugenics Society Papers. *The Mendel Newsletter* (June) no. 14: 9–14.

Armstrong, Esta. 1983. Interview, New York City, Feb. 6.

Arnold, Charles. 1978. "Public Health Aspects of Contraceptive Sterilization." In *Behavioral-Social Aspects of Contraceptive Sterilization*, edited by Sidney Newman and Zanvel Klein. Lexington, Mass: Lexington Books.

Association for Voluntary Sterilization. n.d. (post-1971). A Statement of Purpose and Program. New York: Association for Voluntary Sterilization.

Bachrach, Peter, and Elihu Bergman. 1973. *Power and Choice: The Formation of American Population Policy*. Lexington, Mass.: Lexington Books.

Bambara, Toni Cade. 1970. "The Pill: Genocide or Liberation." In *The Black Woman*, edited by Toni Cade Bambara. New York: New American Library.

Barclay, William, Joseph Enright, and Reid Reynolds. 1970. Population Control in the Third World. *NACLA Newsletter* 4, no. 8 (Dec.): 1–19.

Barker-Benfield, G. J. 1976. *The Horrors of the Half-Known Life: Male At- titudes Toward Women and Sexuality in Nineteenth-Century America.* New York: Harper and Row.

Barnes, Allan C. and Frederick Zuspan. 1958. Patient Reactions to Puer- peral Surgical Sterilization. *American Journal of Obstetrics and Gyne- cology* 75: 65–71.

Bell, Daniel. 1976. *The Cultural Contradictions of Capitalism.* New York: Basic Books.

Bell, Winifred. 1983. *Contemporary Social Welfare.* New York: MacMillan.

Bergman, Elihu, and Peter Bachrach. 1973. "Participation and Conflict in Making American Population Policy: A Critical Analysis." In *Aspects of Population Growth Policy,* edited by the Commission on Population Growth and the American Future. Washington, D.C.: U.S. Government Printing Office.

Blair, Gwenda. 1977. Abortion Rights: What Went Wrong. Mimeograph.

Blake, Judith. 1975a. "Coercive Pronatalism and American Population Pol- icy." In *Population Studies,* 2d ed., edited by Kenneth Kammeyer. Chi- cago: Rand McNally.

Blake, Judith. 1975b. "Population Policy for Americans: Is the Government Being Misled?" In *Population: Dynamics, Ethics, and Policy,* edited by Priscilla Reining and Irene Tinker. Washington, D.C.: American Asso- ciation for the Advancement of Science.

Bluestone, Barry, and Bennett Harrison. 1982. *The Deindustrialization of America.* New York: Basic Books.

Bock, Gisela. 1983. Racism and Sexism in Nazi Germany: Motherhood, Compulsory Sterilization, and the State. *Signs* 8, no. 3 (Spring): 400–21.

Bogue, R. and D. W. Sigelman. Sterilization Report Number 3: Continuing Violations of Federal Sterilization Guidelines by Teaching Hospitals in 1979. Washington, D.C.: Public Citizens Health Research Group.

Bossard, James. 1934. "The New Public Relief and Birth Control." Phila- delphia: Pennsylvania Birth Control Federation.

Boston Globe. 1982. "Reagan Says Economy is Beginning an Upturn." A4, July 7.

Bram, Susan. 1978. Women and Children First or How Pop Planning Fucked Over Mom." *Heresies* 6: 65–73.

Breines, Wini. 1982. *Community and Organization in the New Left: The Great Refusal.* New York: Praeger.

Breines, Wini, and Linda Gordon. 1983. The New Scholarship on Family Violence. *Signs* 8, no. 3 (Spring): 490–31.

Brown, Richard. 1979. *Rockefeller's Medicine Men*. Berkeley: University of California Press.

Buck v. Bell. 1927. 274 US 200.

Bumpass, Larry, and Harriet Presser. 1972. Contraceptive Sterilization in the United States: 1965 and 1970. *Demography* 9, no. 4 (Nov.): 531–48.

Califano, Joseph. 1981. *Governing America*. New York: W. W. Norton.

CARASA News. 1978. Population Controllers Plan Ahead. 2, no. 10. New York: Committee for Abortion Rights and Against Sterilization Abuse.

Caress, Barbara. 1975. Sterilization: Women Fit To Be Tied. *Health/PAC Bulletin* 62 (Jan.–Feb.): 1–13.

Carlson, Jody, and George Vickers. 1982. "Voluntary Sterilization and Informed Consent: Are Guidelines Needed?" New York: *UMC News*.

Center for Disease Control. 1979. *Surgical Sterilization Surveillance: Tubal Sterilization, 1970–1975*. Washington, D.C.: Department of Health, Education, and Welfare.

CESA Papers. A collection of documents of the Committee to End Sterilization Abuse, which are in the author's possession.

Chase, Allan. 1977. *The Legacy of Malthus*. New York: Knopf.

Commission on Population Growth and the American Future. 1972. *Population and the American Future*. New York: Signet.

Committee for Abortion Rights and Against Sterilization Abuse. 1979. *Women Under Attack: Abortion, Sterilization Abuse, and Reproductive Freedom*. New York: Committee for Abortion Rights and Against Sterilization Abuse.

Conrad, Peter. 1975. The Discovery of Hyperkinesis: Notes on the Medicalization of Deviant Behavior. *Social Problems* 23, no. 1 (Oct.): 12–21.

Cox, D. R. 1970. *The Analysis of Binary Data*. London: Methuen.

Cutright, Phillips, and Frederick Jaffe. 1977. *Impact of Family Planning Programs on Fertility: The U.S. Experience*. New York: Praeger.

Darity, William, Castellano Turner, and H. Jean Thiebaus. 1971. "Race Consciousness and Fears of Black Genocide. *Population Reference Bureau Section* 37 (June): 5–12.

Davis, Angela. 1981. *Women, Race, and Class*. New York: Random House.

Demerath, Nicholas J., II. 1976. *Birth Control and Foreign Policy*. New York: Harper and Row.

Devine, Joel. 1983. Fiscal Policy and Class Income Inequality: The Distributional Consequences of Governmental Revenues and Expenditures in the United States, 1944–1976. *American Sociological Review* 48, no. 5: 606–22.

Domhoff, William G. 1979. *The Powers That Be: Processes of Ruling-Class Domination in America*. New York: Vintage Books.

Donovan, Patricia. 1976. Sterilization and the Poor: Two Views on the Need for Protection from Abuse. *Family Planning/Population Reporter* 5, no. 2 (Apr.): 28–30.

Dreifus, Claudia. 1978. "Sterilizing the Poor." In *Seizing Our Bodies: The Politics of Women's Health Care*, edited by Claudia Dreifus. New York: Random House.

Drinnon, Richard. 1961. *Rebel in Paradise; A Biography of Emma Goldman*. New York: Harper and Row.

Duvall, Henrietta, Karen Goodreau, and Robert Marsh. 1982. Aid to Families with Dependent Children: Characteristics of Recipients in 1979. *Social Security Bulletin*, 45 (Apr.): 3–9, 19.

Edwards, Richard. 1979. *Contested Terrain: The Transformation of the Workplace in the Twentieth Century*. New York: Basic Books.

Ehrenreich, Barbara, and Deirdre English. 1973. *Complaints and Disorders: The Sexual Politics of Sickness*. Old Westbury, N.Y.: The Feminist Press.

Ehrenreich, Barbara, and Deirdre English. 1978. *For Her Own Good: 150 Years of the Experts' Advice to Women*. Garden City, N.Y.: Anchor/Doubleday.

Ehrlich, Paul. 1968. *The Population Bomb*. New York: A Sierra Club–Ballantine Book.

Eisenstein, Zillah. 1982. "The Sexual Politics of the New Right: Understanding the 'Crisis of Liberalism' for the 1980s." In *Feminist Theory: A Critique of Ideology*, edited by Nannerl Keohane, Michelle Rosaldo, and Barbara Gelpi. Chicago: University of Chicago Press.

Eliot, Johan, Robert Hall, J. Robert Willson, and Carolyn Houser. 1970. "The Obstetrician's View." In *Abortion in a Changing World*, edited by Robert Hall. New York and London: Columbia University Press.

Erie, Steven, Martin Rein, and Barbara Wiget. 1982. "Women and the Reagan Revolution: Thermidor for the Social Welfare Economy." In *Families, Politics and Public Policy*, edited by Irene Diamond. New York: Longman.

Family Planning Digest. 1972a. 1, no. 1. "Simpler Methods Boost Public Acceptance."

Family Planning Digest. 1972b. 1, no. 1. "They Want Good Birth Control, Can't Get It."

Family Planning Digest. 1974a. 3, no. 3. "Programs Served 3.2 Million in 1973; Provided Counties, Agencies Increase."

Family Planning Digest. 1974b. 3, no. 6. "Experts Agree 2% Growth Rate is Too High, But Differ on Means to Slow Growth."

Feldman, J. G., S. Ogra, J. Lippes, and H. Sultz. 1971. Patterns and Purposes of Oral Contraceptive Use by Economic Status. *American Journal of Public Health* 61: 1089.

First International Eugenics Congress. 1912. "First International Eugenics Congress, London, July 24th to 30, 1912." London: Eugenics Education Society.

Fitzgerald, F. Scott. 1925. *The Great Gatsby.* New York: Charles Scribner's Sons.

Ford, Kathleen. 1978. Contraceptive Use in the U.S., 1973–1976. *Family Planning Perspectives* 10: 264–69.

Fuge, Denise. 1983. Interview, New York City, Oct. 10.

Gamble, Clarence J. 1933. Clarence J. Gamble Papers. Letter to his uncle, Ray Chapin, Nov. 20, 1933. Francis A. Countway Library of Medicine, Boston.

Gamble, Clarence J. 1935. Clarence J. Gamble Papers. Solicitation letter from Pennsylvania Birth Control Federation, Philadelphia, dated Feb. 23, 1935. Francis A. Countway Library of Medicine, Boston.

Gelles, Richard, ed. 1979. *Family Violence.* Beverly Hills: Sage.

George, Susan. 1977. *How the Other Half Dies: The Real Reasons for World Hunger.* Montclair, N.J.: Allanheld, Osmun, and Co.

Gerzowski, Michelle, S. Berlucchi, and Allan Dobson. 1981. Medicaid Sterilizations (1976–1980). Paper presented at annual meeting, American Public Health Association. Nov. 1–15.

Gilder, George. 1981. *Wealth and Poverty.* New York: Basic Books.

Glazer, Nathan and Irving Kristol, eds. 1976. *The American Commonwealth—1976.* New York: Basic Books.

Goethe, C. M. 1945a. Clarence J. Gamble Papers. Letter to Mrs. Ralph K. Miller, May 4, 1945. Francis A. Countway Library of Medicine, Boston.

Goethe, C. M. 1945b. Clarence J. Gamble Papers. Letter to Dr. C. J. Gamble, May 7, 1945. Francis A. Countway Library of Medicine, Boston.

Goldmann, Lucien. 1969. *The Human Sciences and Philosophy.* London: Jonathan Cape.

Gomel, Victor. 1978. Profile of Women Requesting Reversal of Sterilization. *Fertility and Sterilization* 30: 39–41.

Gordon, Linda. 1976. *Women's Body, Women's Right.* New York: Penguin.

Gordon, Linda. 1981. The Long Struggle for Reproductive Rights. *Radical America* 15: 75–88.

Gordon, Linda and Allen Hunter. 1978. Sex, Family, and the New Right. *Radical America* 12 (Nov. 1977–Feb. 1978).

Gough, Ian. 1979. *The Political Economy of the Welfare State*. London: MacMillan.

Gould, Stephen J. 1981. *The Mismeasure of Man*. New York: W. W. Norton.

Gray, Virginia. 1974. "Women: Victims or Beneficiaries of U.S. Population Policy?" In *Political Issues in U.S. Population Policy*, edited by Virginia Gray and Elihu Bergman. Lexington, Mass.: Lexington Books.

Gruening, Ernest H. 1977. *Many Battles*. New York: Liveright.

Hacker, Andrew, ed. 1983. *U/S*. New York: Penguin.

Haller, Mark M. 1963. *Eugenics: Hereditarian Attitudes in American Thought*. New Brunswick, N.J.: Rutgers University Press.

Hanushek, Eric. A. and John E. Jackson. 1977. *Statistical Methods for Social Scientists*. New York: Academic Press.

Hardin, Garrett. 1968. The Tragedy of the Commons. *Science* 162: 1243–48.

Harrington, Michael. 1984. "U.S.'s Next Economic Crisis." *New York Times*, E23, Jan. 15.

Higham, John. 1965. *Strangers in the Land: Patterns of American Nativism, 1860–1925*. New York: Antheneum.

Hirsch, Henry A., M. Mall, and Burritt Haag. 1976. Changing Methods of Sterilization as Influenced by Laparoscopy. *Journal of Reproductive Medicine* 16: 325–28.

Hirsch, Jerry. 1984. Personal communication regarding folder entitled "Hitler and the Jews, Clippings, 1933–1934." Harry H. Laughlin Collection. Northeast Missouri State University, Kirksville.

Hochschild, Arlie. 1983. Is the Left Sick of Feminism? *Mother Jones* 8, no. 5 (June): 56–58.

Hofstadter, Richard. 1959. *Social Darwinism in American Thought*. New York: George Braziller.

Holmes, Helen, Betty Hoskins, and Michael Gross, eds. 1981. *Birth Control and Controlling Birth: Women-Centered Perspectives*. Clifton, N.J.: Humana Press.

Hout, Michael. 1979. Age Structure, Unwanted Fertility, and the Association between Racial Composition and Family-Planning Programs: A Comment on Wright. *Social Forces* 57 (June): 1387–92.

Hunter, Allen. 1981. In the Wings: New Right Organization and Ideology. *Radical America* 15, nos. 1, 2 (Spring): 113–40.

Huntington, Samuel. 1975. "Welfare Shift." In *The Crisis of Democracy: A Report on the Governability of Democracy to the Trilateral Commission*, edited by Michael Crozier, Samuel Huntington, and Joji Watanuki. New York: New York University Press.

Huntington, Samuel. 1976. "The Democratic Distemper." In *The American Commonwealth—1976*, edited by Nathan Glazer and Irving Kristol. New York: Basic Books.

Jaffe, Frederick. 1974. Short-Term Costs and Benefits of United States Family-Planning Programs. *Studies in Family Planning* 5, no. 3 (Mar.): 98–105.

Jones, James. 1981. *Bad Blood: The Tuskegee Syphilis Experiment.* New York: The Free Press.

Katz, Michael and Mark Stern. 1980. History and the Limits of Population Policy. *Politics and Society* 10, no. 2: 225–45.

Kammeyer, Kenneth, ed. 1975. *Population Studies: Selected Essays and Research*, 2d ed. Chicago: Rand McNally.

Kammeyer, Kenneth, Norman Yetman, and McKee McClendon. 1975. "Family-Planning Services and the Distribution of Black Americans." In *Population Studies: Selected Essays and Research*, 2d ed., edited by Kenneth Kammeyer. Chicago: Rand McNally.

Kennedy, David M. 1970. *Birth Control in America: The Career of Margaret Sanger.* New Haven and London: Yale University Press.

Krauss, Elissa. 1975. Hospital Survey on Sterilization Policies. New York: American Civil Liberties Union.

Kristol, Irving. 1978. *Two Cheers for Capitalism.* New York: Basic Books.

Lader, Lawrence. 1971. *Breeding Ourselves to Death.* New York: Ballantine Books.

Lappe, Frances Moore, and Joseph Collins. 1977. *Food First: Beyond the Myth of Scarcity.* Boston: Houghton Mifflin.

Laughlin, Harry. 1930. *"The Legal Status of Eugenical Sterilization."* Washington: Eugenics Record Office.

Lekachman, Robert. 1979. Troubles of the Welfare State. *Dissent* (Fall): 414–29.

Lewit, Sarah. 1973. Sterilizations Associated with Induced Abortion: JPSA Findings. *Family-Planning Perspectives* 5, no. 3: 177–82.

Lipsky, Michael. 1980. *Street-Level Bureaucracy.* New York: Russell Sage Foundation.

Littlewood, Thomas. 1977. *The Politics of Population Control.* Notre Dame, Ind.: University of Notre Dame Press.

Ludmerer, Kenneth. 1972. *Genetics and American Society.* Baltimore: Johns Hopkins University Press.

Luker, Kristin. 1975. *Taking Chances: Abortion and the Decision Not to Contracept*. Berkeley: University of California Press.

Magaziner, Ira, and Robert Reich. 1982. *Minding America's Business: The Decline and Rise of the American Economy*. New York and London: Harcourt Brace Jovanovich.

Malthus, Thomas. 1967. *An Essay on the Principle of Population*. London: Dent; New York: Dutton.

Mamdani, Mahmood. 1972. *The Myth of Population Control: Family and Caste in an Indian Village*. New York and London: Monthly Review Press.

Marksjarvis, Gail. 1977. "The Fate of the Indian." *National Catholic Reporter*, 2–5, May 27.

Mass, Bonnie. 1976. *Population Target*. Toronto: Latin American Working Group.

McCarthy, John and Mayer Zald. 1977. Resource Mobilization and Social Movements: A Partial Theory. *American Journal of Sociology* 82: 1212–41.

McCoy, D. 1968. The Emotional Reaction of Women to Therapeutic Abortion and Sterilization. *Journal of Obstetrics and Gynaecology*, British Commonwealth 75: 1054.

McDougall, William. 1923. "The Correlation Between Native Ability and Social Status." In *Second International Congress of Eugenics. Scientific Papers. Vol. II: Eugenics in Race and State*. Baltimore: Williams and Wilkins.

McGarrah, Robert, Jr. 1975. Sterilization Without Consent: Teaching Hospital Violations of HEW Regulations. Washington, D.C.: Public Citizen Health Research Group.

McLaughlin, Loretta. 1983. "When a Doctor Confronts the Church." *Boston Globe Magazine*, Jan. 23.

Measham, Anthony R., A. A. Hatcher, and C. B. Arnold. 1971. Physicians and Contraception: A Study of Perceptions and Practices in an Urban Southeastern U.S. Community. *Southern Medical Journal* 64: 499.

Medical Tribune. 1977. "Genocide Charged by Indian M.D. Investigator." Aug. 24.

Medical Tribune. 1978. "Letter to the Editor from David M. Priver, M.D." Apr. 12.

Medical World News. 1973. "Sterilization Guidelines: 22 Months on the Shelf." Nov. 9.

Michaelson, Karen. 1981. "Introduction: Population Theory and the Political Economy of Population Processes." In *And the Poor Get Children: Radical Perspectives on Population Dynamics*, edited by Karen Michaelson. New York and London: Monthly Review Press.

Mohr, James. 1978. *Abortion in America: The Origins and Evolution of National Policy, 1800–1900*. New York: Oxford University Press.

Monthly Vital Statistics Report. 1983. "Births, Marriages, Divorces, and Deaths for 1982." 31, no. 12 (Mar. 14). Hyattsville, Md.: Public Health Service.

Muller, Charlotte. 1978. Insurance Coverage of Abortion, Contraception, and Sterilization. *Family-Planning Perspectives* 10, no. 2: 71–77.

Murray, Douglas. 1982. The Abolition of El Cortito, the Short-Handled Hoe: A Case Study in Social Conflict and State Policy in California Agriculture." *Social Problems* 30, no. 1 (Oct.): 26–39.

National Center for Health Statistics. 1979. *National Survey of Family Growth, Cycle II, Tape Contents Manual.* Washington: U.S. Department of Commerce, National Technical Information Services, PB-297 346.

National Conference on Social Welfare. 1978. *Families and Public Policies in the United States, Final Report of the Commission.* Washington, D.C.: National Conference on Social Welfare.

National Women's Health Network. 1980. *Sterilization: Resource Guide 9.* Washington D.C.: National Women's Health Network.

New York Times. 1983. "Many Women in Poll Value Jobs as Much as Family Life." A1, 66. Dec. 4.

New York Times. 1983. "Reagan Assails Great Society." Dec. 4.

New York Times. 1983. " 'Hi Tech' is No Jobs Panacea, Experts Say." A1, 28, Sept. 18.

New York Times. 1970. "President Signs Birth Curb Bill." A1, Dec. 27.

New York Times. 1980. "Sterilization of Teenage Women Haunting Virginia Decades Later," A16, Mar. 7.

New York Times. 1970. "President Signs Birth Curb Bill." A1, Dec. 27.

New York Times Index 1973: A Book of Record. 1974. New York: The New York Times Company.

Notestein, Frank. 1970. Zero Population Growth. *Population Index* 36: 444–51.

N.O.W.–New York. 1977. "Letters to Thomas J. Cuite, Vice Chairperson, New York City Council," Apr. 15.

N.O.W.–New York. 1978. *Fact Sheet on Sterilization Abuse.* New York: National Organization for Women.

Oberschall, Anthony. 1973. *Social Conflict and Social Movements.* Englewood Cliffs, N.J.: Prentice-Hall.

Olden, Marian. 1946. "The ABC of Human Conservation." Birthright, Inc.

Paul, Julius. 1968. The Return of Punitive Sterilization Proposals: Current Attacks on Illegitimacy and the AFDC Program. *Law and Society Review*, 3, no. 1 (Aug.): 77–106.

Pennsylvania Birth Control Federation. 1934. "Mr. & Mrs. Taxpayer—" Philadelphia: Pennsylvania Birth Control Federation, n.d. (probably 1934). Clarence J. Gamble Papers. Francis A. Countway Library of Medicine, Boston.

Pennsylvania Birth Control Federation. 1936. "Birth Control Is . . ." Clarence J. Gamble Papers. Francis A. Countway Library of Medicine, Boston.

Perelman, Michael. 1977. *Farming for Profits in a Hungry World: Capital and the Crisis in Agriculture*. Montclair, N.J.: Allanheld, Osmun, and Co.

Petchesky, Rosalind Pollack. 1984. " 'Reproductive Choice' in the Contemporary United States: A Social Analysis of Female Sterilization." In *And the Poor Get Children: Radical Perspectives on Population Dynamics*, edited by Karen Michaelson. New York and London: Monthly Review Press.

Petchesky, Rosalind Pollack. 1981. *Abortion and Woman's Choice: The State, Sexuality, and Reproductive Freedom*. New York and London: Longman.

Piotrow, Phyllis. 1973. *World Population Crisis*. New York: Praeger.

Piven, Frances Fox, and Richard A. Cloward. 1971. *Regulating the Poor: The Functions of Public Welfare*. New York: Vintage.

Piven, Frances Fox, and Richard A. Cloward. 1979. *Poor People's Movements: Why They Succeed, How They Fail*. New York: Vintage.

Piven, Frances Fox, and Richard A. Cloward. 1982. *The New Class War*. New York: Pantheon Books.

Placek, Paul J., and Gerry E. Hendershot. 1974. Public Welfare and Family Planning: An Empirical Study of the "Brood Sow" Myth. *Social Problems* 21: 659–73.

Plaskon, Vera. 1982. "Sterilization Techniques." In *The International Encyclopedia of Population*, edited by John Ross. New York: The Free Press.

Poma, Pedro A. 1980. Why Women Seek Reversal of Sterilization. *Journal of the National Medical Association* 72, no. 1: 41–48.

Popenoe, Paul, and Ellen M. Williams. 1934. Fecundity of Families Dependent on Public Charity. *American Journal of Sociology* 49, no. 2 (Sept.): 214–20.

Population Council. 1958. *Annual Report: 1958*. New York: Population Council.

Population Council. 1968. *Annual Report, 1968*. New York: Population Council.

Population Council. 1978. *The Population Council. A Chronicle of the First Twenty-five Years, 1952–1977*. New York: Population Council.

Population Reports. 1978. "M/F Sterilization." *Population Reports*, no. 2 (March). Baltimore: Johns Hopkins University.

Population Reports. 1980. "Female Sterilization." *Population Reports*. Ser. C, no. 8 (Sept.). Baltimore: Johns Hopkins University.

Presser, Harriet B. 1969. The Role of Sterilization in Controlling Puerto Rican Fertility. *Population Studies* 5, no. 3: 343–61.

Presser, Harriet B. 1978. "Contraceptive Sterilization as a Grass-roots Response: A Comparative View of the Puerto Rico and United States Experience." In *Behavioral-Social Aspects of Contraceptive Sterilization*, edited by Sidney Newman and Zanvel Klein. Lexington, Mass.: Lexington Books.

Rapp, Rayna. n.d. Family and Class in Contemporary America: Notes Toward an Understanding of Ideology. Manuscript.

Reed, James. 1978. *From Private Vice to Public Virtue: The Birth Control Movement and American Society Since 1830*. New York: Basic Books.

Relf v. Weinberger et al. 1974. 372 F.Supp 1196 (D. D.C. 1974).

Rodriguez-Trias, Helen. 1978. Sterilization Abuse. *Women and Health* 3 (May–June): 10–15.

Rodriguez-Trias, Helen. 1983. Interview, New York City, Mar. 27.

Rosenfeld, Bernard, Sidney Wolfe, and Robert McGarrah. 1973. "A Health Research Group Study of Surgical Sterilization: Present Abuses and Proposed Regulations." Washington, D.C.: Public Citizen Health Research Group.

Roth, Julius. 1974. "Some Contingencies of the Moral Evaluation and Control of Clientele: The Case of Hospital Services." In *Human Service Organizations*, edited by Yeheskel Hasenfeld and Richard English. Ann Arbor, Mich.: University of Michigan Press.

Rothschild, Emma. 1981. Reagan and the Real America. *New York Review of Books*, Feb. 5, 1981: 12–18.

Rowbotham, Sheila. 1974. *Hidden from History: Rediscovering Women in History from the Seventeenth Century to the Present*. New York: Pantheon Books.

Ruzek, Sheryl B. 1978a. Planned Parenthood and the Women's Health

212 *References*

Movement. Address to Planned Parenthood Physicians' meeting, San Diego, Calif. Oct. 24.

Ruzek, Sheryl B. 1978b. *The Women's Health Movement.* New York: Praeger.

Sanger, Margaret. 1926. The Functions of Sterilization. *Birth Control Review*, Oct.: 299.

Savage, Wendy. 1982. Taking Liberties with Women: Abortion, Sterilization, and Contraception. *International Journal of Health Services* 12, no. 2: 293–307.

Schirmer, Jennifer. 1982. *The Limits of Reform: Women, Capital, and Welfare.* Cambridge, Mass.: Schenkman.

Schwendinger, Herman, and Julia Schwendinger. 1974. *The Sociologists of the Chair.* New York: Basic Books.

Schultz, Theodore. 1982. *Investing in People: The Economics of Population Quality.* Berkeley: University of California Press.

Schwyhart, W. R., and S. J. Kutner. 1973. A Reanalysis of Female Reactions to Contraceptive Sterilization. *Journal of Nervous and Mental Disease* 156: 354–70.

Shapiro, Thomas, William Fisher, and Augusto Diana. 1983. Family Planning and Female Sterilization in the United States. *Social Science and Medicine* 17, no. 23: 1847–55.

Shorrock, Tim. 1983. Atari Moves to Asia. *Multinational Monitor* 4, no. 4 (Apr.): 11–13.

Sigelman, Daniel. 1981. *Health Research Group Report Number 4 on Sterilization Abuse of the Nation's Poor under Medicaid and Other Federal Programs.* Washington, D.C.: Public Citizen Health Research Group.

Silver, Morton. 1971. Survey of Private Physicians—Summary of Initial Findings. Paper presented at the American Public Health Association Annual Meeting, Minneapolis, Minn., Oct. 11.

Simon, Julian. 1981. *The Ultimate Resource.* Princeton, N.J.: Princeton University Press.

Smart, Carol, and Barry Smart. 1978. "Women and Social Control." In *Women, Sexuality, and Social Control,* edited by Carol Smart and Barry Smart. London, Henley, and Boston: Routledge and Kegan Paul.

Stamm, Karen. 1983. Interview, New York City, Feb. 5.

Steinfels, Peter. 1979. *The Neoconservatives: The Men Who Are Changing America's Politics.* New York: Simon and Schuster.

Steinmetz, Suzanne, and Murray Straus, eds. 1974. *Violence in the Family.* New York: Harper and Row.

Tietze, Christopher. 1946. Report #2-18th. September 1946. Clarence J. Gamble Papers. Francis A. Countway Library of Medicine, Boston.

Tilly, Charles. 1978. *From Mobilization to Revolution*. Reading, Mass.: Addison Wesley.

U.S. Bureau of the Census. 1976. Money Income in 1975 of Families and Persons in the U.S. *Current Population Reports*, ser. P-60. Washington, D.C.: U.S. Government Printing Office.

U.S. Bureau of the Census. 1981. *Statistical Abstract of the United States, 1981*. Washington, D.C.: U.S. Government Printing Office.

U.S. Bureau of the Census. 1982. *Consumer Income 1981*, ser. P-60. Washington, D.C.: U.S. Government Printing Office.

U.S. Commission on Civil Rights. 1983. *A Growing Crisis: Disadvantaged Women and Their Children*. Washington, D.C.: U.S. Government Printing Office.

U.S. Department of Health and Human Services. 1980. *Five-Year Plan for Family-Planning Services and Population Research*. Washington, D.C.: U.S. Government Printing Office.

U.S. Department of Health, Education, and Welfare. 1978. Contraceptive Utilization in the United States: 1973 and 1976. *Advanced Data*, 36. Washington, D.C.: U.S. Government Printing Office.

U.S. General Accounting Office. 1976. Medical Research Involving Indian Subjects. B-164031 (5). Washington, D.C.: U.S. Government Printing Office.

U.S. Office of Management and Budget. 1983. *Special Analyses of the Budget of the United States, 1984*. Washington, D.C.: U.S. Government Printing Office.

U.S. Senate Committee on Appropriations. 1972. Departments of Labor and Health, Education, and Welfare Related Agencies Appropriations for Fiscal Year 1973. *Hearings before a Subcommittee of the Committee on Appropriations*. Washington, D.C.: U.S. Government Printing Office.

U.S. Senate Subcommittee on Health. 1973. *Hearings on Quality of Health Care—Human Experimentation, 1973, Part 4*. 93rd Cong. 1st sess. Washington, D.C.: U.S. Government Printing Office.

Useem, Michael. 1984. *The Inner Circle: Large Corporations and the Rise of Business Activity in the U.S. and U.K.* New York: Oxford University Press.

Vanessendelft, William. 1978. A History of the Association for Voluntary Sterilization: 1935–1964. Unpublished Ph.D. thesis, University of Minnesota.

Vaughan, Denton, and Gerald Sparer. 1974. "Ethnic Group and Welfare Status of Women Sterilized in Federally Funded Family Planning Programs, 1972. *Family Planning Perspectives* 6 (Fall): 224–29.

Velez, Carlos G. 1978. *Se Me Acabo La Cancion*: An Ethnology of Cultural Disruption and Social Network Disengagement Among Nonconsenting Sterilized Mexican Women in Los Angeles. Paper presented at the International Congress of Anthropological and Ethnological Sciences, New Delhi, India, Dec. 10–18.

Washington Post. 1980. "Over 7,500 Sterilized by Virginia." A1, 20, Feb. 23.

Washington Star. 1980. "Some Doctors Are Critical of Sterilization Guidelines." 2, June 22.

Weisbord, R. 1973. Birth Control and the Black American: A matter of genocide? *Demography* 10: 571–90.

Weissman, Steve. 1970. Why the Population Bomb Is a Rockefeller Baby. *Ramparts* 8 (May): 42–47.

Westoff, Charles. 1975. "The Commission on Population Growth and the American Future." In *Sociology and Public Policy*, edited by Mirra Komarovsky. New York: Elsevier.

Westoff, Charles, and Norman Ryder. 1977. *The Contraceptive Revolution*. Princeton, N.J.: Princeton University Press.

Westoff, Charles, and Elise Jones. 1977a. Contraception and Sterilization in the United States, 1965–1975. *Family Planning Perspectives* 9 (July–Aug.): 153–57.

Westoff, Charles, and Elise Jones. 1977b. The Secularization of U.S. Catholic Birth Control Practices. *Family Planning Perspectives* 9 (July–Aug.): 203.

Westoff, Charles, and James McCarthy. 1979. Sterilization in the United States. *Family Planning Perspectives* 11 (Nov.–Dec.): 147–52.

Williams, Doone, and Greer Williams. 1978. *Every Child a Wanted Child: Clarence James Gamble, M.D., and His Work in the Birth Control Movement*, edited by Emily P. Flint. Distributed by Harvard University Press for the Francis A. Countway Library of Medicine, Boston.

Wilson, Elizabeth. 1977. *Women and the Welfare State*. London: Tavistock.

Wood, H. Curtis. 1973. The Changing Trends in Voluntary Sterilization. *Contemporary Obstetrics and Gynecology* 1, no. 4: 31–39.

Woolf, Virginia. 1966. *Three Guineas*. New York: Harcourt Brace Jovanovich (originally published 1938).

World Agriculture Research Project. 1969. The Political Economy of Food and Agriculture. *International Journal of Health Services* 10, no. 1: 161–69.

Wright, Gerald. 1978. Racism and the Availability of Family-Planning Services in the United States. *Social Forces* 56 (June): 1087–98.

Zatuchini, Gerald, ed. 1970. *Post-Partum Family Planning.* New York: McGraw-Hill.

Zeitlin, Maurice. 1980. "On Class, Conflict and the State: An Introductory Note." In *Class, Class Conflict and the State,* edited by Maurice Zeitlin. Cambridge, Mass.: Winthrop.

Index

Abortion: defunding of, 125; reduced availability of, 189; use of, by poor, 124–25. *See also* Hyde Amendment
Abortion and Woman's Choice, 10
Acosta, Guadalupe, 4–5, 90
Ad Hoc Advisory Committee on Sterilization Guidelines, 138
Agency for International Development, 16, 81, 82
Aid to Families with Dependent Children, and family planning assistance, 112
Alford, Robert, 19–20
Allen, Garland, 46, 47
American Civil Liberties Union, 93, 138
American College of Obstetricians and Gynecologists, 87, 114, 140
American Eugenics Society (AES), 45–47. *See also* Osborn, Frederick
Armstrong, Esta, 138, 139, 140, 151, 161
Association for Human Betterment, 55. *See also* Association for Voluntary Sterilization
Association for Voluntary Sterilization (AVS), 24, 54–59; and OEO guidelines, 114; origins of, 54–55; and sterilization guidelines, 139

Bachrach, Peter, 22, 23–24, 63, 83
Bambara, Toni Cade, 84
Barker-Benfield, C. J., 11
Barnes, Allan, 134
Bell, Alexander Graham, 35
Berelson, Bernard, 68–69
Bergman, Elihu, 22, 23–24, 63, 83
Birth control, 8; differences in practices of, 9–10
Birth control movement, and the depression, 50–51
Birthright, Inc., 55. *See also* Association for Voluntary Sterilization
Black, Eugene, 75
Black liberation movement, and government-sponsored family planning, 84
Boas, Franz, 60
Bossard, James, 49–50
Bronk, Detlev, 64, 65, 75
Buck, Carrie and Doris, 3–4
Buck v. Bell, 3
Bumpass, Larry, 94, 126
Burden, Carter, 141
Burden Bill, 141–42

217